8 WEEKS
TO A
BETTER
RELATIONSHIP

Canadian Cataloguing First Publication Date: December 2012
Second Publication Date: October 2013
ISBN-13: 978-1492860891   ISBN-10: 1492860891
Ted Kuntz, Lee Johnson and Rowan Johnson
8 Weeks to a Better Relationship
1. Relationships   2. Self-improvement
3. Self-Help / Personal Growth / Happiness

Layout, design and typography by Lee Johnson
Edited by Lee Johnson, Literary Consultant

Cover design by Lee Johnson

8 WEEKS TO A BETTER RELATIONSHIP

TED KUNTZ
M.Ed.

LEE JOHNSON
B.A. Hons

ROWAN JOHNSON
M.A.

DEDICATION

*This book is dedicated
to all who strive to become
better people
and better partners*

INTRODUCTION

Welcome to *8 Weeks to a Better Relationship*. Although this book focuses primarily on intimate (romantic) relationships, we sincerely believe this book will help improve the quality of all your relationships.

In our experience, two factors prevent most people from achieving the kind of relationships they desire:

    (1)   a lack of knowledge about how to be in an intimate relationship;

    (2)   a lack of skill to behave in ways that contribute to a happy and healthy relationship.

The good news is both of these conditions are treatable. By the time you've completed *8 Weeks to a Better Relationship* we're confident you will have the knowledge and skills needed to allow you to enjoy more rewarding and satisfying relationships not only in your closest, most intimate relationship, but also in all areas of your life.

WHAT MAKES THIS BOOK DIFFERENT

First, *8 Weeks to a Better Relationship* is more than simply a source of information about relationships. It is also a <u>workbook</u> where you will participate in a number of exercises, both individually and together.

Thirdly, it is a <u>journal</u> where you will record your thoughts and reflections as you engage the material. We offer you plenty of opportunities to 'pause and ponder'. These are places where we invite you to record your thoughts and feelings as you reflect upon your relationships and your life.

Therefore, *8 Weeks to a Better Relationship* is essentially three books in one.

In addition, this book demands that you <u>take action</u>. Its focus is on changing thoughts, attitudes and behaviors. This is important because achieving better relationships won't occur simply by reading this (or any other) book. To improve your relationships, you must *do something different than you've been doing*. Indeed, one of the principles upon which this book is founded is this:

If you want something you've never had before,

you must be willing to do something you've never done before.

If nothing changes, nothing changes!

The primary goals of 8 Weeks to a Better Relationship is to have you <u>thinking</u> and <u>behaving</u> in new ways. Success occurs when you identify the ideas and behaviors that don't work for you, and take action towards ideas and behaviors that <u>do</u> work for you.

Finally, this work is different because it's written jointly by three guys. While each of us is trained in psychotherapy, we bring our unique ideas and skills because of our different ages, experiences and backgrounds. We fully acknowledge that having a female co-author would have been hugely valuable, and we also believe that both men and women will gain valuable insights and benefit from the perspectives we bring.

PURCHASE A COPY FOR YOUR PARTNER

In order to receive the greatest benefit from this 8 week journey, we encourage you to purchase two copies of this book: one for you, and one for your partner.

We recommend this because in our many years as marriage and family therapists and as partners in our own relationships, we discovered that efforts to improve a relationship are much more effective when both individuals participate in the commitment at the same time.

By having two books, both of you are able to read and work with the material at the same time. It also allows the two of you to read and work at your own pace, yet be in alignment with one another as you walk the journey toward greater intimacy. Additionally, when both of you engage the material at the same time you demonstrate to one another your very real commitment to improving your relationship. This sends a powerful message to your partner and avoids the potential of one person thinking he or she is doing all the work.

In our early testing of the book, many couples reported excellent results from not only reading the book at the same time, but also actually taking turns to read to one another. Try it and see what that experience is like for you.

Finally, by each having your own book, you are able to record your own thoughts and feelings privately as you engage the material. This enables the two of you to read the chapters and complete the exercises in your own time, and feel a sense of privacy to enable you to be completely honest when completing the exercises.

(The time will come later in the book for you to share information, but initially it's important to feel your personal thoughts are safe).

If you dislike writing in a book (as some do), or if you are using an electronic version of the book, you can download the entire set of exercises from our website *www.8weekstoabetterrelationship. com.* The exercises are free and can be downloaded as many times as you wish.

A final note: While Ted mostly took the lead writer role, all three authors collaborated fully and frequently. In the text we sometimes make use of the 'royal we', meaning it's our consensus. And while we might sometimes say things like, 'being marriage therapists', this would apply mainly to Ted, to a lesser extent, Lee, and endorsed by Rowan. Each makes a special contribution, and it is not our intent to misrepresent ourselves in any way.

We are fully confident that within eight weeks, if you use this book correctly and are committed to following through with action, you will have made a significant shift from where you are now, both as individuals and as a couple.

We hope you find the process as valuable as it has already been for each of us.

Ted Kuntz   M.Ed.
Lee Johnson   B.A. Hons
Rowan Johnson   M.A.

Vancouver, British Columbia, Canada
and Chattanooga, Tennessee, USA; Dec 2012

THANK YOU

We would like to express our sincere appreciation to the many generous people who contributed to this book by way of suggestions, support, and encouragement.

We especially want to acknowledge the many hundreds of couples who shared their journey with us over the years. Together, we discovered how to create better relationships. You have helped to develop a path for those who follow you.

A special thank you to Rita deGraaf, Linda Denis, and the members of the *Wine, Women & Words* book club: Susan Verver, Suzanna Gray (and Laurie), Rohini Gandhi, Susan Hayto (and Steve), Lana Cullis, and Nancy Stephenson. Your input and enthusiasm for this project is most appreciated.

INDEX

IMPORTANT: HOW TO USE THIS BOOK

8 Weeks—One Week at a Time! That's all it takes to have a better relationship. We promise.

We know you're eager to get started, but please take the time to read this section carefully. It's very important.

Each chapter contains information and exercises designed to help you to improve your relationship, and is intentionally designed to be read one chapter per week.

So, for the next eight weeks, we suggest you dedicate just one day or evening per week to the task of working on your relationship. It's easier if you make it a regular date—say, every Monday night. Read the assigned chapter, then complete the exercises contained in the chapter.

You may find it helpful to re-read each chapter a number of times to fully appreciate its content.

While you may be eager to push ahead and read the entire book at once, we encourage you to be patient. You will derive greater benefit from reading *8 Weeks to a Better Relationship* in weekly sections and applying the concepts to your relationship incrementally, than reading the book quickly from cover to cover.

This book is more than simply information about healthy relationships. It is a carefully designed process for creating the kind of relationships you want.

While this book has been written with 'couple relationships' (i.e. romantic/intimate) in mind, it is by no means limited to that. *8 Weeks to a Better Relationship* contains information and skills to improve all of your relationships.

HOW TO ENGAGE YOUR PARTNER

If you have come to this material before your partner, (perhaps it's you who took the initiative and made the decision to purchase it), it's important to invite your partner to *work with you* to improve your relationship.

Your chances of success will be greatly improved if both you and your partner are working on enhancing your relationship at the same time.

If you're wondering how to engage your partner in this journey of bettering your relationship, we offer the following suggestions:

1. Approach your partner from a position of love

Love energy is the best way to win the co-operation of your partner. Tell your partner that you love him/her and want to improve your relationship with them. Explain to your partner that you've discovered this book, *8 Weeks to a Better Relationship*, and would like to use it as a resource to assist the two of you.

It would work best if <u>each of you could have your own copy of the book</u> so that you can engage the material together. Another option would be to photocopy the blank exercise pages so that both of you can work on them at the same time while retaining your own private thoughts.

But, whether they agree to this or not, ask your partner to review the book, (even if it's just reading this introduction), and decide if he or she is willing to work with you on improving your relationship at this time.

2. Don't justify your desire to improve your relationship

Simply let your partner know that you want your relationship to be better; that you believe this will make both of you happier. Having a better relationship depends on <u>both of you</u> wanting that.

3. Imagine your partner saying 'yes'

Use your creative energy to imagine a *positive* response. As you'll discover later, we explore how your imagination is a very powerful tool.

4. Use encouragement

It's very necessary that your partner participates in this journey willingly and by his or her own choice. There is no benefit in using coercion as a way to get your partner to work on your relationship with you.

(Coercion can look like anger, resentment, withholding, threats, sarcasm, or pressure of any sort). Resist the urge, and instead be encouraging and inviting.

5. Be prepared to start the process without your partner

If your partner is reluctant to participate in the process at this time, be willing to start anyway. Let your partner know you are committed to improving your relationship. Ask them to provide you with feedback as to the changes they notice as you begin the work. As you read *8 Weeks to a Better Relationship*, share with your partner what you are learning.

When your partner witnesses improvement in your relationship, and experiences some of the benefits of that, he or she will be more likely to want to participate in the process also.

6. Expect to have fun

The process of improving your relationship is invigorating. Learning and growing is exciting for you individually as well as for your relationship.

So, get excited about the possibility of a better relationship! Enthusiasm and excitement are contagious. Infect your partner with your excitement!

CHANGE TAKES COURAGE

We applaud you for the courage to pick up this book and committing to making changes to improve your relationship. We know the process of change takes courage. In a previous #1 best-selling book, *How to Escape your Comfort Zones*, co-author Lee Johnson describes the challenges most people experience while attempting to make change. You may find it useful to read this too.

People almost always find it difficult to move from a place that is familiar, to a place that is unfamiliar. As a consequence, most people behave in the same ways even though these behaviors no longer work for them. And yet, change is crucial to our success, both individually and collectively. Without change, nothing progresses. Renowned Jungian psychologist James Hillman once stated,

You have to give up the life you have,

in order to get the life that's waiting for you.

A definition of insanity we appreciate is this one –

Insanity is doing the same thing

and expecting a different outcome

This analogy is also useful: when you are climbing a ladder, you need to take your foot off one rung in order to move it to a higher one. Have you been doing the same things over and over again in your relationship and expecting a different outcome? Now is the time to do something different!

The first step in making a change is to acknowledge what is and is not working in your relationship. The next step is to take actions to improve those aspects of your relationship that aren't working. No significant change will occur unless you make an 'honesty assessment' of your relationship up front. Examine all aspects of it and be completely honest with yourself. You can't change what you don't acknowledge.

However, with information, encouragement and vision, positive change is definitely possible. *8 Weeks to a Better Relationship* provides the information and encouragement you need to experience a better relationship.

CRISIS AS OPPORTUNITY

Is there a crisis that has motivated you to pick up this book? For most, the word 'crisis' has a negative association. Yet this doesn't have to be the case. A crisis is also an opportunity: a situation where you have been pushed to the edge of the cliff and *have* to make a decision.

You may have heard motivational speakers say that the two characters making up the Chinese word for 'crisis' represent elements that signify both 'danger' and 'opportunity'.

While this is now widely regarded as misperception[1], the

---

1   Chinese symbol and explanation courtesy of http://www.pinyin.info/chinese/crisis.html

principle is certainly worth embracing: that a crisis is both a danger and an opportunity at the same time.

Danger   Opportunity

Why is this so? Because change is so difficult for most people, it often requires some kind of crisis to force it to the forefront. A crisis is frequently the catalyst that challenges people to make important changes in their life. A crisis therefore can be an important and powerful ally.

Author Carolyn Myss[2] sums it up:

People are far more motivated to begin

an inner journey as a result of a crisis,

than when all is right with their world.

Carolyn Myss

In a relationship, a crisis may present itself in a number of ways. It may show up as someone having an affair. It may show up as an emotional illness; for example, depression is often an

---

2   http://www.myss.com/

indication of an underlying crisis. A crisis may show up as a major loss such as a death in the family, a job loss, emigration, losing a beloved pet, or an 'empty nest' as a result of one's children leaving home.

If you have been motivated to make changes in your relationship because of a crisis, we invite you to be grateful for the crisis. While this may seem an unusual way of thinking, we have come to appreciate that a crisis has the potential to become a valuable gift.

A crisis can serve as a 'wake up call'. A crisis can bring into focus areas of one's life that have long been avoided or neglected.

A crisis can sometimes be the agent of change that sets you on to the road to health and happiness again. For example, we have worked with many couples where an affair became the event that inspired them to seek a better relationship.

So, instead of using a crisis as an excuse to be depressed and feel victimized, we encourage you to *shift your perspective* and see the crisis not as something negative, but something positive that has been put into your life in order for you to learn a positive lesson.

Ask yourself questions such as, "*What is this crisis meant to teach me?*" and, "*How is this crisis serving me now?*" Consider how this crisis might make you into a stronger and wiser person.

See this crisis as a gift to enlighten you and improve your life. See your crisis as *the reason why* you were attracted to reading and using this book.

People don't move until the pain of not moving
becomes greater than the pain of moving.

Tanis Helliwell

LET'S GET STARTED!

It's time to get you started on your journey to a better relationship.

As with any journey, you'll need to bring certain items with you. If you were taking a journey in the mountains you would need a compass, map, water and food. Our journey to a better relationship also requires that you to bring along certain items. In Week 1 we identify the items you need for your journey toward a better relationship.

There's no better time to start than right now. So, let's begin with Week 1 .

~WEEK 1:

If you do what you have always done,
You will get what you have always got.
If nothing changes, nothing changes.

WELCOME TO WEEK ONE.

Congratulations on beginning your journey. We guarantee that you will emerge at the end of this eight-week process a better person and a better partner.

We're excited to get going. So, let's dig right in.

ATTRIBUTES OF AN INTIMATE RELATIONSHIP

Our journey to a better relationship begins with the question: What qualities or attributes are necessary to experience an intimate relationship? We believe three attributes are essential:

1. Worthiness
2. Choice
3. Responsibility

During this week we will explore each of these attributes in depth. As part of this exploration we'll ask you to complete some exercises that enable you to assess to what extent these three attributes exist in your relationship. There is a direct connection between the presence of these attributes and a healthy and happy relationship.

THE FIRST ATTRIBUTE: WORTHINESS

In his book *The Psychology of Romantic Love*, Nathaniel Branden writes: *"If we do not love ourselves, it is almost impossible to believe fully that we are loved by someone else."*

Branden's words are a fitting way to introduce our first attribute—worthiness. By worthiness we mean the belief that you are worthy and deserve to experience intimacy, joy and love in your life.

Unless and until you love yourself, you will not be able to accept the love of another. Branden explains:

"No matter what our partner does to show that he or she cares, we do not experience the devotion as convincing because we do not feel lovable to ourselves."

Our core belief about our 'lovability' determines the kind of relationship we are able to experience. As marriage therapists, we have observed many people who held core beliefs that they did not deserve love or were unlovable. These beliefs are serious impediments to experiencing intimacy in relationships.

Having a core belief of unworthiness reminds us of a joke attributed to comedian George Burns. Burns announced that he *"would not join any club that would accept him as a member"*.

While this statement was meant as humor, we've noticed many people holding a similar attitude. They won't be in a relationship with anyone who will accept them. They believe there must be something wrong with the person who would choose to love them.

As a consequence, they often find themselves with partners who judge and reject them. Sadly, because of their core beliefs, rejection and judgment is more familiar and comfortable than acceptance.

And so: if you possess a core belief of being unworthy, it will be impossible for you to experience a better relationship until you change this core belief.

The attribute of 'worthiness' is absolutely essential if you wish to experience a healthy and intimate relationship.

HOW WORTHY DO YOU FEEL?

The following exercise will help you assess the degree to which you perceive yourself as worthy. Read each statement and indicate your level of agreement or disagreement by circling the appropriate number. Be completely truthful, even if it hurts. In general, rely on your gut feelings and the first answer that comes to mind. Don't ponder too much.

When you have finished, add your scores together and enter the total in the space provided. A key is provided below to help you understand your results. (Don't cheat by looking up the answers in advance! There are no 'rights' or 'wrongs'. And you'd only be reducing the value of this exercise—and this book.)

1. **I deserve to enjoy a truly wonderful relationship.**
    Disagree   1   2   3   4   5   Agree

2. **It's possible to have all I want in life.**
    Disagree   1   2   3   4   5   Agree

3. **Some people have worse relationships than I do, therefore I should be happy with what I have.**
    Disagree   5   4   3   2   1   Agree

4. **I expect too much out of life generally.**
    Disagree   5   4   3   2   1   Agree

5. I'm worthy of happiness, joy and abundance in my life.

    Disagree 1   2   3   4   5   Agree

6. I deserve to have whatever I desire and will continue to strive to have this.

    Disagree 1   2   3   4   5   Agree

7. If my current relationship doesn't work for me, I know I'll find a relationship that does.

    Disagree 1   2   3   4   5   Agree

8. I should feel grateful to have this relationship even though it's not what I truly want.

    Disagree 5   4   3   2   1   Agree

9. All relationships are difficult.

    Disagree 5   4   3   2   1   Agree

10. I like who I am and I desire to become even better.

    Disagree 1   2   3   4   5   Agree

Total _____

SCORING

Add up your scores. The higher your score, the more you perceive yourself as worthy. The lower your score, the less worthiness you experience at this time. A score of 40 or higher indicates you have the attribute of worthiness necessary to enjoy an intimate relationship. A belief in your own worthiness is essential if you want to experience a truly joyful and intimate relationship.

THE ROLE OF 'AGREEMENTS'

In his book *The Four Agreements*, Don Miguel Ruiz uses the word 'agreements' to describe our core beliefs. He suggests that all of us enter into agreements with others and that these agreements are a mutual understanding about who we are. We've noticed that people who are in satisfying relationships have an agreement with others that declares, *"I'm worthy to receive love"* and, *"I am lovable just as I am"*. Agreements such as these contribute to healthy relationships. We call these kinds of agreements <u>self-expanding beliefs</u>.

SELF-EXPANDING BELIEFS

In order to experience an intimate and joyful relationship, it's essential you have a positive 'agreement' about who you believe yourself to be. Self-expanding beliefs are perceptions and agreements we hold that make it possible to experience peace, joy and happiness in life. Without a core belief of worthiness, your efforts to create a better relationship will be undermined by you at either a conscious or unconscious level.

PAUSE AND PONDER

Below is a list of sample core beliefs, both positive and negative. Use this list to help identify beliefs about yourself you currently hold. When you identify a core belief that limits your perception of who you are or what you are entitled to experience, mark these beliefs for change. Rewrite these statements to reflect the belief you would like to have about yourself.

When you have written your list of self-expanding beliefs in the section below titled *Some Positive Beliefs About Myself*, copy them from your book and paste the list in a visible location—a bathroom mirror, a refrigerator door, or a kitchen cupboard. Read your list often during the next eight weeks, and really think about each self-expanding belief. Feel each one deep inside. This action will help you adopt these new self-expanding beliefs.

Some Positive Beliefs about myself:

- I'm worthy just the way I am.
- I deserve love.
- I deserve happiness.
- I can have whatever I desire.
- I can make choices for myself.
- I have power to change my life.

- I am lovable just the way I am.
- I am worthy of peace, joy, and happiness in my life.
- I can do it.
- Everything that is happening to me is ultimately for my highest good.
- I'm worthy of abundance in my life.
- There is enough time, energy, and money to have what I desire.

Some Negative Beliefs about myself:

- I'm not good enough.
- I'm not lovable.
- I'm not attractive enough.
- I'm not worthy.
- I don't deserve good things.
- I should be happy with what I have.
- I need to be different in order to be accepted and loved.
- I deserve to be neglected, rejected, and ignored.
- I need to earn love.

CHANGING ONE'S CORE BELIEFS

Our core beliefs can and do exert a powerful influence over our lives. In order to improve your relationship, it is necessary to recognize and change any beliefs that are self-limiting.

Most people resist changing their core beliefs. They mistakenly assume their beliefs simply 'are' and therefore cannot or should not be changed.

We invite you to consider the perspective offered in Ruiz's book, *The Four Agreements*. He states that beliefs are simply ideas we have been taught about our self, others, and the world around us. These ideas are useful only to the degree they help us to live happy and fulfilling lives. Truth is simply what you believe <u>at this time</u>. Your 'truth' ought to continually evolve as you acquire new information and experiences in life.

HOW PERCEPTION INFLUENCES BEHAVIOR

Co-author Lee Johnson spent many years working as a copywriter and creative director with some of the world's leading advertising agencies. He helped create campaigns with the clear intent of changing the consumer's beliefs about a product. This is essentially what advertisers do. The basis of advertising is simple—change the belief, and you change the buying behavior of the consumer.

Most people see ads in magazines or watch commercials on television and don't realize the enormous effort that goes into formulating an advertising strategy. The finished ad or commercial is the creative execution of a very carefully considered strategy to change the consumers' beliefs.

Let Lee give you an example of a commercial he was involved with.

"The advertising agency I was working for was hired to stimulate sales of a new dishwashing liquid; let's call it Product A. Consumer surveys indicated that a competitive dishwashing liquid, Product B, was believed to be more powerful than Product A. When asked why they held this belief, the rationale given was because product B was thicker than product A, and therefore it must be stronger and last longer.

"The Product A brand development team went back to the drawing boards to make improvements. After many weeks, however, it was found that product re-formulations were too expensive. They were stumped. Finally, a junior member of the team made a simple suggestion: 'Why not just make the hole smaller?'

"And that's exactly what the product development specialists did.

"When consumers tried to use the 'new, improved' Product A, they had to squeeze harder to make the liquid come out.

"Conclusion? Their perception was that the liquid was thicker, and therefore it must be stronger and would last longer.

"The agency launched a new advertising campaign simply calling it 'New and Improved', and used a couple of consumer testimonials. Within a few months, sales of Product A had overtaken those of Product B."

This example illustrates the incredible power of beliefs. Change someone's belief (even if that belief is not based in fact!), and you change their behavior.

This principle works whether you are buying dishwashing liquid or trying to improve your relationship. Change your beliefs, and your behavior will change as well.

Best of all, changing your belief is something that is completely within your power to do. You can do it right here, right now. A simple change in attitude can change the way you perceive yourself and everyone around you.

Below is an opportunity to write out positive beliefs you have or would like to have about yourself.

POSITIVE BELIEFS ABOUT MYSELF

The greatest discovery of my generation
is that a person can alter their life
simply by altering their attitude.

William James, 1902

Remember to paste this list in a visible location, and to read it often—including upon waking in the morning and before going to sleep at night.

- Feel them deep inside.
- Believe them.
- Behave as if these statements are already true.

THE SECOND ATTRIBUTE: CHOICE

One core belief critical to creating a better relationship is the belief, "*I have a choice*".

Having a choice is one of the most important attributes of an intimate relationship. In order to improve your relationship, it is vital that you participate in your relationship by choice. While this may seem obvious, we've encountered many people who feel they have no choice in their relationship—usually because of religious, social, financial, or other reasons.

Sadly, in our experience, the perception of having 'no choice' is very common. Many people believe once they make the decision to marry, their choice of partner cannot be changed. Some people are even of the opinion that this state of 'no choice' is necessary for the relationship to succeed. While such ideas are common in even the most liberal of societies, our experience has led us to believe that the perception of no choice leads to unhappy and unhealthy relationships. Living with the perception of no choice not only undermines the capacity of people to fully enjoy and appreciate their relationship, but also impedes their capacity to enjoy life.

Rather than enhance the relationship, people often become reactive and defensive to the degree they believe they have no choice. Consequently, relationships lose their joy when the people feel powerless. The perception of 'no choice' also tends to evoke feelings of resentment.

We believe it is crucially important that both individuals feel they are in the relationship by choice; each and every day.

Do you feel that you have a choice to be in your relationship?

CHOICE OR NO CHOICE?

Take a few minutes to consider to what extent you feel you have *choice* in your present relationship. Read the statements below and indicate your level of agreement or disagreement by circling the appropriate number. At the end, add up your scores and write the total in the space provided. A key is provided to help you interpret your results.

CHOICE-NO CHOICE QUESTIONNAIRE

1.   **I'm in this relationship because I choose to be.**

     Disagree   1   2   3   4   5   Agree

2.   **The only reason I stay in this relationship is because I am forced to stay.**

     Disagree   5   4   3   2   1   Agree

3.   **I'm enjoying my partner and don't feel stifled or stuck in the least.**

     Disagree   1   2   3   4   5   Agree

4.   **I know I could end this relationship and I would still be OK.**

     Disagree   1   2   3   4   5   Agree

5. **I stay in this relationship because it's against my religion to leave.**

    Disagree   5   4   3   2   1   Agree

6. **Choice? There is no such thing as 'choice' when you have children, a mortgage, and other obligations.**

    Disagree   5   4   3   2   1   Agree

7. **If I won a lottery I'd be out of here in a flash!**

    Disagree   5   4   3   2   1   Agree

8. **Sometimes I wish my partner would have an affair, then I could justify leaving.**

    Disagree   5   4   3   2   1   Agree

9. **Like it or not, a marriage is forever.**

    Disagree   5   4   3   2   1   Agree

10. **My family/ friends/ colleagues wouldn't support me if I separated or got divorced.**

    Disagree   5   4   3   2   1   Agree

Your Total Score _____

SCORING

Add up your scores. The higher your score, the more choice you feel you have in your relationship. The lower your score, the less choice you experience in your relationship. A score of 40 or more indicates there is sufficient choice in your relationship to support a healthy future.

THE INSTITUTION OF MARRIAGE

Some people believe that ending a relationship when it isn't working, is simply wrong. Our culture, our religions, and our media have sent this message for generations, and as a result it's not uncommon for people to think they have failed themselves, their families and their religion if a relationship ends.

We'd like to challenge this perspective. We've noticed when people are unhappy in a relationship, they eventually get sick— emotionally sick as well as physically sick. This is because it's difficult to be living a life that isn't working—especially when you believe you have no power to change it.

It's our perception that these feelings of failure are because society seems to be more committed to *the institution of marriage* than to *the health and well-being of the people in the marriage*.

And so, rather than continue to suffer when a relationship isn't working and you genuinely feel you've done all you can to make it work, the best action might be to <u>end</u> the relationship. From our experience, it is a failure to stay in something that isn't working. And that's true for both parties involved.

Clients often ask us what is the rate of success of marriage therapists. Our answer is that it depends on how you measure success. If success is measured by the number of marriages continuing, we're successful about half the time. If success is measured by both people living happier and healthier lives, then we're successful almost all of the time.

One of the problems with marriage is that most of us select our life partner while in our early twenties. Some are even younger when they make this important decision. Are we wise enough at this stage of life to make a decision about who is a suitable life partner? Statistics are pretty clear: about 50% of marriages end in divorce—that's almost 1 in 2.

It's also not surprising to hear that research suggests that if an individual waits until age twenty-eight to get married, he or she reduces the likelihood of divorce by about half. This is pretty obvious: the more mature we are, the more likely we are to make good decisions. But for most of us, waiting is not an option: when we're in love, we like to believe it's forever.

Unfortunately, the pressure to find a mate often comes from all sides: family, friends, and the media. All these can push a person to make this important decision before they are ready.

Truth is, marriage isn't the only kind of relationship that can fail. While some recent surveys indicate that divorce rates are decreasing, these may be misleading because in many countries the proportion of married couples has also been steadily decreasing over the past 20 years while common-law unions are becoming more numerous. (*Huffington Post, August 2012*)

Married or unmarried, people don't ever stop changing. Not one of us is the same person now as we were as we were a decade or two ago. Our interests change. Our goals change. Our perspectives change. Even what we enjoy and are attracted to, changes over time.

And all of these changes affect our relationships.

Perhaps it is necessary to re-evaluate our societal and cultural expectations that have us choose a partner in our relative youth, then expect this relationship continue regardless of the health, safety or benefit.

Possibly we also need to reconsider the kind of vows we make when getting married. Most make a vow to love someone "till death do us part". We think a different commitment might serve individuals and marriages better. More about this later.

Daphne Rose Kingma, author of *The Future of Love* states that our current societal paradigm requires that love have four components. She explains that for love to be sanctioned in our society as love, it must be *daily, domestic, exclusive* and *forever.*

Kingma then goes on to describe some loving relationships that are successful even though they contain none of these four components. Her book makes an important contribution to challenging our understanding of what love is.

Our hope is that you continue in your relationship because you truly want to, rather than because you believe you have no choice. We hope that your relationship is based on desire rather than fear, duty or obligation.

FEAR, DUTY, OR OBLIGATION

In our experience it's common for people to stay in a relationship out of fear, duty or obligation. Fear of what might happen if they changed or ended their relationship. Fear of what friends, neighbors and other family members might say.

Fear of being alone. Fear of not being able to cope on one's own. Fear of financial loss. Fear of failure.

Fear of your partner's success with another. Fear of being rejected by children. Even fear of God's judgment.

What is true is that your relationship is unlikely to be rewarding or intimate if it is based in fear. This is because fear paralyses, constricts and causes us to defend ourselves. Fear activates our primal brain response of fight or flight.

And if 'fleeing' the relationship is not an option, the natural result of a fear-based relationship is that it becomes a fight.

LOVE AND FEAR

What emotion is your relationship based upon—love or fear? This may be a difficult question for you to answer at this time. Neale Donald Walsch provides some insight:

There are only two energies
at the core of the human experience:
love and fear.

Love grants freedom, fear takes it away.

Love opens up, fear closes down.

Love invites full expression, fear punishes it.

By this measure you can know whether someone

is loving you, or fearing you.

Do not look to what they say. Look to what they do.

Neale Donald Walsch

Conversations with God

IS YOUR RELATIONSHIP LOVE-BASED OR FEAR-BASED?

If you want to create a better relationship it is important that your relationship is built on a foundation of love. The following statements describe love-based and fear-based relationships. Read each set of statements and, being totally honest with yourself, identify those statements that best describe your current relationship. The following statements are based on fear:

- I'm not good enough.
- I can't manage on my own.
- I don't trust myself or others.
- It's not my place to make decisions.
- I'm not in control.
- I'm powerless.

- I have no choice.
- I'm afraid to be on my own.
- I can't take care of myself.
- My partner controls everything.
- I can't say no.
- I'm always walking on eggshells.
- I need to be careful with what I say or do.
- I'm constantly worrying in my relationship.

The statements below are based on love:

- I can manage.
- I have choice.
- I can say what I think.
- I create the experiences in my life.
- I'm lovable just the way I am.
- I love myself.
- I nurture myself.
- I can be spontaneous.
- I can take care of myself.
- I can be honest and open about what I think and feel.
- I feel safe.
- I am trusting and confident.
- I am powerful.
- My life is filled with ease and grace.

Which of the above descriptions best describes how you think and feel in your relationship?

Are your answers predominantly love-based or fear-based?

WANT VS. NEED

Another way of recognizing if you are living with choice is to pay attention to the language you use when describing your relationship.

In particular, we invite you to pay attention to the words 'need' and 'want'. Do you describe your relationship in terms of need, or in terms of want? Notice the difference between the following pairs of statements:

- · I need my partner.
- · I want my partner.

- · I need to be married.
- · I want to be married.

- · I need my partner to agree with me.
- · I want my partner to agree with me.

- · I need to stay in this relationship.
- · I want to stay in this relationship.

Do you feel the difference in the emotional tone of the above statements? The energy of *need* is different than the energy of *want*.

The use of the word 'need' may be an indication that you are living without choice. The fact is when you believe that you need something, your basic survival instincts are activated. Then, if what you believe you need doesn't happen, you experience feelings of fear, panic and distress.

Bob's story may help give some insight into the impact of 'need' and 'want':

BOB'S STORY

Bob was married for fifteen years to a woman who held different ideas and values than his own. Bob stayed in his marriage because he believed he needed to make his marriage work. His need was based on religious beliefs and his own commitment to stay married until 'death do us part'.

After years of frustration, loneliness and disappointment, Bob finally decided to end his marriage. Yet he continued to feel guilty for not having made the marriage work. Bob struggled further because he needed to have his ex-wife understand his reasons for ending the marriage. When she didn't understand or accept his reasons, Bob felt frustrated and angry.

A counselor invited Bob to re-assess whether these were true needs or whether he had simply mislabeled his wants as needs. This was a novel idea for Bob. It soon became apparent that he had lived for years under the mistaken notion that he needed his marriage to work; that he needed his partner to understand and agree with him; and that he needed his partner to be happy. When these needs didn't happen, Bob became angry, resentful and scared.

It was liberating for Bob to realize that what he had perceived as needs weren't needs after all. Rather, they were *wants*. Bob wanted his marriage to be successful. Bob wanted his partner to understand him. Bob wanted his partner to be happy.

The shift Bob experienced wasn't just a shift of words. When Bob finally understood each of these considerations as a 'want' rather than a 'need', he felt liberated. He felt lighter, easier and freer.

By recognizing the difference between wants and needs, Bob was able to reclaim the experience of choice in his life.

PAUSE AND PONDER

↔> **What do you currently experience as 'needs' in your relationship?**

↔> **How do you feel when your 'needs' are not met?**

✍ Which of these are not true needs, but actually wants?

✍ Write out each statement as "I want" rather than "I need".

✍ What difference does it make to experience 'needs' as 'wants'?

IT'S NOT A MATTER OF SURVIVAL

When you begin to recognize that what you have labeled as needs are actually wants, you come to the understanding you will survive even if your wants don't occur.

In reality we have few true needs. We need air to breathe, food to eat, and shelter to keep us warm.

We might prefer (want) many things including a good relationship, however we don't *need* these things to survive. In fact, we don't even need most of these things to be happy, though we may think that we do!

LOVE = CHOICE

Love allows your relationship to change and evolve over time. People living in fear-based relationships often feel suppressed. They believe they can't be who they are, or do what they desire, due to their fear. Unfortunately, hiding or suppressing one's fear will not improve matters.

In our collective experience, hiding or burying emotions, pushing down or suppressing or 'de-pressing' one's emotions, invariably leads to the state we commonly call depression. Many experts believe certain kinds of depression are the result of chronically de-pressing one's emotions.

As therapists we also believe that others can sense fear no matter how unspoken or suppressed these feelings may be. Most people instinctively know whether someone is with them because they truly desire to be, or whether they are with them out of a sense of duty or obligation.

As a child, did you have the experience of a sibling or relative tagging along with you because you were told by a parent you had no choice but to play together? How was that experience for you? How did the sense of obligation affect the relationship?

For most people, relationships of obligation are unfulfilling. People often confess that they feel anger and resentment at having no choice.

Naturally the same applies to adult relationships. Love does not thrive where there is anger and resentment or obligation.

THE POWER OF CHOICE

There is little doubt that the freedom to choose enhances a relationship, while the absence of choice tends to restrict a relationship. To improve your relationship it is important you feel you are in it *by choice*, and that you also can access choice.

We believe it is impossible for your relationship to become better while you hold on to the belief that you have no choice.

Best selling author Dr. Wayne Dyer says that, "... *relationships based on obligation lack dignity*". For any relationship to improve, the people within the relationship need to feel strong, dignified and healthy. A healthy relationship is built on the foundation of healthy individuals. A relationship cannot become strong and healthy when the people within the relationship feel powerless and dishonored.

For the next eight weeks we invite you to consider whether you are in your relationship by choice or as a result of duty and obligation.

Your power ends where your fear begins.

Barbara Marciniak
The Path to Empowerment

THE THIRD ATTRIBUTE: RESPONSIBILITY

The third attribute of a healthy relationship is responsibility. This means taking full responsibility for one's life. Once again this attribute may seem obvious. However, we regularly observe people giving away the responsibility for managing their lives. The most common example of this is the belief that someone else is responsible for your happiness.

MAKING SOMEONE ELSE RESPONSIBLE

In our work as therapists it's common to hear people blaming their partner for their unhappiness. *"She makes me so angry!"* … *"It's your fault that I'm so unhappy!"* … *"You insulted me."* At the same time their partner is often frustrated because of his or her inability to 'make' the other person happy. They reassure us they have tried everything. They feel frustrated, discouraged and hopeless. They may even want to give up on the relationship because of their inability to make the other person happy.

Our counsel to these individuals is they are unable to make their partner happy for one simple reason—they don't have enough power. In fact, no one has the power to make another person feel happy or sad. If we were that powerful, we would make everyone happy all the time!

The truth is, all emotions are <u>self</u>-created. No one, other than yourself, is responsible for your happiness or sadness. While another person may contribute to your environment (and you to theirs), your emotional response is <u>your</u> responsibility.

If you make others responsible for your emotional response, you do both yourself and the other person a disservice. This is because when you blame another, you give away your power for something you are ultimately responsible for, and you make someone else responsible who in reality doesn't have the power. This can only lead to frustration and failure.

Our observation is that people become 'crazy' when they take responsibility for something they can't control.

EACH OF US IS RESPONSIBLE FOR OUR OWN HAPPINESS

Abraham Lincoln is reported to have said, *"Most people are about as happy as they make up their minds to be."* He didn't say *"Most people are as happy as their partners make them."* In order to be happy it is necessary to take 100% responsibility for your happiness. This means owning the responsibility for your emotions rather than blaming someone else.

For many people this is an unfamiliar concept. This is because we live in a society where blaming another is often rewarded. In the long term, however, blaming does not serve us well. This is because blame is usually linked to *power*.

The act of blaming another implies that another person had the power to make the situation better (or worse); and while we might feel 'right', or justified, or less guilty by blaming another, the bottom line is that we give away our power when we blame.

Even worse: the act of assigning blame, or making others responsible, invariably causes the relationship to fail.

Accepting blame also damages relationships. By taking responsibility for someone else's emotional response, you prevent them from taking responsibility for themself. You allow them to hold a belief system that enables them to give away their power.

We regularly see this happening with parents of teenagers. By assuming responsibility for ensuring that their teenager's homework is completed, for example, a parent is often surprised when the teen feels and acts with no sense of responsibility.

And why should they, when the parent has taken on that responsibility? The teen may even know instinctively that there is no point in two people taking responsibility for the same thing.

We believe this simple rule prevails in all relationships: There is no point in two people being responsible for the same thing. And if you decide to take responsibility for their life, then don't expect the other person to do the same for you.

'VICTIMITIS'

Ray Woollam, author of two innovative books, *On Choosing With a Quiet Mind* and *Have a Plain Day* believes most people suffer from a condition he calls 'victimitis'. Victimitis occurs whenever we blame someone or something else for our life being the way it is. Woollam claims 'victimitis' has reached epidemic levels in our society.

Victimitis can make people sick. It causes frustration, sadness, powerlessness, and failure. Unfortunately, many people have been trained to be good victims. Most of today's leaders act as if they are victims and powerless over the decisions they make. How many times have you heard a politician or the CEO of a company make the statement: "*I had no choice but to ….raise taxes or lay off workers or (insert your own situation).*"

The truth is that we _always_ have a choice.

Pretending we have no choice does not serve us well. We grow as individuals, and our relationships become healthier when we take responsibility for our lives. Taking responsibility means making statements such as, "*I've reviewed all of the choices before me, and based upon the information I have and my own knowledge and experience, I choose the following option.*"

TAKE 100% RESPONSIBILITY

If you want a better relationship, it's essential you take 100% responsibility for your life. This includes taking responsibility for your happiness and sadness. You need to take ownership of all of your choices—including your choice of feelings.

Feelings don't just happen. They are your response to events and circumstances in life. They are something you create by the meaning you give to life's events.

Your feelings are entirely dependent upon the stories you tell yourself. If you want to change your feelings, change your story.

The degree to which you take responsibility for yourself is the degree you will create happiness and joy in your life. The degree to which you blame others is the degree you will create suffering and powerlessness. We believe that a healthy relationship requires that each person take 100% responsibility for whatever is occurring in the relationship.

In many relationships it is common for people to accept 50% responsibility for whatever is occurring in their lives. Unfortunately, taking 50% of the responsibility means you are 50% powerless to change the situation.

Having only 50% of the power is not workable. If you want to be successful in creating a better relationship, you need to take 100% of the responsibility.

We hope your partner will also take 100% of the responsibility. That way, the relationship will benefit from *both of you* taking full responsibility for working out a better solution.

PAUSE AND PONDER

Take a few minutes to complete the following exercise. This will assist you to identify to what extent the quality of responsibility exists in your relationship. Read the following statements and indicate your level of agreement or disagreement by circling the appropriate number below.

A key is provided at the end to help you to score your results. As before, don't ponder to much.

1. **My unhappiness is mainly due to my partner.**

   Disagree   5   4   3   2   1   Agree

2. **I'm 100% responsible for the happiness I experience in my life.**

   Disagree   1   2   3   4   5   Agree

3. **When we're fighting I wait for my partner to make the first move to reconcile.**

   Disagree   5   4   3   2   1   Agree

4. **When I'm unhappy I look at what I'm doing to create my unhappiness.**

   Disagree   1   2   3   4   5   Agree

5. **I have a tendency to blame others when I'm angry.**

   Disagree   5   4   3   2   1   Agree

6. **I regularly monitor my happiness and sadness and make changes to improve my life.**

        Disagree   1   2   3   4   5   Agree

7. **I regularly feel angry and resentful.**

        Disagree   5   4   3   2   1   Agree

8. **I believe I am powerful and am the creator of my experience.**

        Disagree   1   2   3   4   5   Agree

9. **Other people make me feel bad about myself.**

        Disagree   5   4   3   2   1   Agree

10. **I can only be insulted with my permission.**

        Disagree   1   2   3   4   5   Agree

Your Score _____

SCORING

Add up your scores. The higher your score, the *more* responsibility you take in your relationship. The lower your score, the *less* responsibility you take. A score of 40 and above means you are contributing positively to the health of your relationship.

HOW DID YOU DO?

In the spaces below, write down your scores for each of the above exercises. As we have seen, *Worthiness*, *Choice* and *Responsibility* are the three ingredients we believe are necessary for a healthy relationship. Remember, higher scores (i.e. closer to 40) are better than low scores (closer to zero).

Ingredient	Recommended	Your Score
Worthiness	40	----------
Choice	40	----------
Responsibility	40	----------

How did you do? Which ingredients are well developed? Which ingredients require some attention? If you want a better relationship it's important that *all three of the qualities*—worthiness, choice and responsibility—are well developed.

We've discovered that without these three ingredients, no amount of hard work, time or money will significantly improve your relationship. If one or more of these ingredients is seriously lacking, you need to make a commitment right now to improve these aspects; either on your own or with someone's help.

Perhaps it may be necessary to access some professional counseling—because more than being essential components of a healthy relationship, each of these ingredients also represents an important aspect of a healthy individual and a healthy life.

POSITIVE AFFIRMATIONS

One way that you can gradually increase the presence of these ingredients in your life, is to create the intention and regularly affirm the presence of these qualities in your life.

Below is a list of positive affirmations relating to our work this week. You may want to add to the list by identifying affirmations that reflect the areas of your relationship in need of support.

Make a commitment to read the affirmations daily throughout the eight weeks.

You can use the following statements to start your list of Positive Affirmations:

Worthiness:

I am worthy of peace, joy and happiness in my relationship.

Choice:

I always have choice in my life, no matter what the circumstances. At any moment, I can activate my power of choice.

Responsibility:

I am 100% responsible for all my thoughts, feelings and behaviors. If I don't like any aspect of my life, it is my responsibility to change it.

NEXT WEEK: CLARIFYING YOUR DREAM

In Week 2, our focus will be to assist you to clarify your dream for a better relationship. We will do this by asking you to describe what your ideal relationship looks and feels like.

After working with many couples we know that to improve your relationship you need to clearly describe what it is you want to experience in your relationship.

PAUSE AND PONDER

> What ideas stood out for you this week?

➭ **What ideas were new to you?**

➭ **What ideas were challenging or difficult for you to accept or understand?**

➭ **What did you learn about yourself?**

✐ **What did you learn about your partner?**

CONGRATULATIONS!

You have completed the **first week** of your journey toward a better relationship.

~WEEK 2:

Everything you see in your life
has been created twice.
First in someone's mind,
then in physical form.

WELCOME TO WEEK TWO.

Last week we identified the attributes that must be present to experience a healthy and intimate relationship. These attributes are:

- Worthiness
- Choice
- Responsibility

You also completed a number of exercises to enable you to assess the degree each of these attributes is present in your relationship. Finally, you committed yourself to improving these qualities in your relationship. This week we assist you to clearly identify and describe your ideal relationship.

CLARIFYING YOUR DREAM

In order to make positive change, it is necessary to have a clear vision of *what* you want to change, as well as what you want to change *to*. You need to be able to answer a vital question: What will be different as a result of change?

The process of making change requires that two questions be answered. These questions are:

- What do I want?
- How will I create what I want?

FOCUSING ON WHAT WORKS

One of the basic tenets of this book is to focus on the positive. Specifically, our focus will be on two important questions: *"What is working now?"* and, *"What do you want to experience?"*

Our intention is that we spend as little time or energy as possible focusing on the negative aspects of your relationship. After all, since we can't chance a single thing about what's happened in the past, what's the point of spending time and energy on it? Change happens *now*.

All your power is in the present moment; in the *now*.

Focusing on the negative isn't helpful or productive... and yet, focusing on the positive is unfamiliar to most people. We've noticed that when a relationship begins to flounder, most couples will focus their attention on what isn't working in the relationship.

"You're always watching TV!"

"You never spend time with the kids; it's just work, work, work!"

"That damn dog gets more attention than I do!"

Most people can more easily generate a list of what is not going well, than what is going well. Ted noticed in his counseling practice that a couple will usually spend, if he lets them, a considerable amount of time and energy sharing the faults of their partner or the shortcomings of the relationship.

Focusing on what *isn't* working, however, does not contribute to positive change. Instead, focusing on the negative aspects of the relationship can have the effect of discouraging partners and pushing a couple even further apart.

THE PRINCIPLE OF FOCUS

From our counseling work we have come to appreciate that one's focus is critical to success. We've discovered that constructive change is more likely to occur when individuals focus on what they want to achieve, rather than on what they don't want in their lives. With this in mind, our focus this week will be on answering questions such as:

"What is my ideal relationship?"

"What does it look like?"

"What does it feel like?"

You will be asked to complete a number of exercises to help you identify what your ideal relationship looks and feels like. By focusing your attention on what you want in your relationship, you increase the likelihood of realizing (making real) your goal. We are utilizing the following principles:

Where attention goes, energy flows!

and:

Wherever you focus your attention
will determine what you experience.

If you focus your attention on the negative aspects of your life, you will unquestionably experience more negativity. Likewise, if you focus your attention on the positive aspects of your life, you will enjoy more positive experiences. Seems rather obvious, doesn't it? The importance of focus cannot be overestimated. The direction you are pointed, determines where you go. What you focus your attention on, will determine what you experience. It's that simple.

LESSONS FROM A PROFESSIONAL RACE CAR DRIVER

During an international modified car racing competition in Vancouver, Ted was given the opportunity to work with one of the professional drivers who shared some wisdom from his profession. He explained:

> *"If a driver should lose control of his vehicle, and the car is headed toward the wall, the driver needs to focus all of his attention on where he wants the car to go, rather than where the car is going.*
>
> *"This means the driver looks for an opening in the field of cars and focuses all of his attention on that opening. The result is that the car will move toward the opening.*
>
> *"If the driver focuses his attention on avoiding the wall, he'll crash into it every time."*

This principle also applies to the direction you are headed in your relationship. If you focus your attention on what isn't working in your relationship (the wall), you will experience just that—a relationship that isn't working.

If you focus your attention on what is working, and keep focusing on what a successful relationship looks like (the openings), you increase the likelihood of experiencing a more successful relationship.

The bottom line is this—your experience is determined by the focus of your attention. In order to make positive changes in your relationship, you must pay attention to your focus.

Unless you change your direction,
You will end up where you are headed.

PAUSE AND PONDER

Let's see if this principle is true for you.

➣ **What has been the focus of your attention over the last six months?**

➣ **As a result of this focus, what have you experienced in the last six months?**

☜ Now that you understand the principle of attention, where will you direct your focus now?

☜ What aspects of your relationship are working well? List them here, or on a separate sheet of paper if you need to.

WHY IDENTIFY YOUR IDEAL RELATIONSHIP?

You might wonder why it is important to identify your ideal relationship. There are four reasons for this.

Firstly, as described above, your focus determines what you experience in life. By focusing on your ideal relationship, you increase the likelihood of creating an ideal relationship.

Secondly, identifying your preferences gives you a benchmark by which to assess your present relationship at this time. It gives you a way to determine how successful you are in your present relationship.

Thirdly, it assists you to identify those aspects of your relationship you might wish to make better.

Finally, identifying what you desire in a relationship is necessary to determine whether your present relationship is viable. Just as you are becoming clearer on what you want to experience in your relationship, so too is your partner.

This clarity will allow you and your partner to answer an important question: "*Do we want the same things?*"

DO YOU SHARE THE SAME VISION?

In order for your relationship to be successful, it is important to determine whether you and your partner want the same relationship. Is there a reasonable degree of overlap in your respective visions for an ideal relationship?

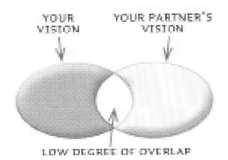
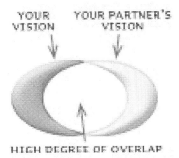

YOUR VISION   YOUR PARTNER'S VISION   YOUR VISION   YOUR PARTNER'S VISION

LOW DEGREE OF OVERLAP   HIGH DEGREE OF OVERLAP

On the left, there is a *low degree of overlap* between your vision (i.e. the preferences you have for a relationship) and that of your partner (i.e. what works for him/her). A low degree of shared vision means the two of you have different dreams and goals for a relationship.

When there is a large amount of overlap, as in the right side of the diagram, there is a *high degree of shared vision*. The two of you have similar dreams and goals for a relationship.

The larger the area of overlap, the more the two of you share a common dream. The smaller the area of overlap, the less the two of you share a common dream.

Determining the degree of overlap or shared vision is an important exercise for all couples to complete. The reason for this is simple: in working with couples, we regularly notice that individuals in less than satisfying relationships often have low levels of overlap. The individuals hold different dreams.

Obvious examples are when one partner wants to have children, while the other does not. Or, one partner wants to have a monogamous relationship, and the other would like a number of sexual partners at the same time.

Less obvious examples exist as well. Differences in priorities regarding finances, friendship, the involvement of extended family, and style of parenting are aspects of a relationship where the amount of overlap is important. These differences can be more pronounced in cross-cultural or interracial relationships, where there is a significant age differential between partners, or where the partners have had very different family experiences growing up. Sometimes, there are pronounced differences in values and spirituality.

BRAD AND MARY

Brad and Mary both said they loved each other very much, yet they were struggling in their relationship. The major area of struggle seemed to be in decision-making. As part of the work of counseling, Ted asked Brad and Mary to describe their preferred style of decision-making.

Mary described wanting to be in a relationship where she was an equal partner and had a right of veto in all important decisions. She really wanted a relationship where two people made decisions together.

When Ted asked Brad to describe his preferred style of decision-making, he reported that his dad always made the important decisions in his parents' marriage, and that this had worked well.

He believed when two people can't agree, someone needs to *be the boss*. In his ideal relationship, he was the boss.

What became clear was that both Brad and Mary believed passionately in their own preferred style of decision-making. Unfortunately, they didn't share the same style.

Result? This couple was destined to struggle unless one or both would be willing to change their preferred style to match or accommodate the other's style.

SHARED VISION IS NEVER STATIC

As we have seen, the more overlap in the vision, the more viable the relationship. The less overlap, the less viable the relationship. It's also important to recognize that a couple can have a high degree of overlap at one stage of their relationship and a smaller degree of overlap at a later stage. This is because people's needs and desires and circumstances change constantly.

If two people are to create a happy and healthy relationship, it is important to determine whether their vision for the relationship is similar both now and into the foreseeable future. It matters little if two people experienced a high degree of overlap in the past. The question is, do they have a shared vision now and going forward?

We have worked with many couples where both agreed that the degree of overlap in their visions during an earlier stage of their relationship was significant. They shared many of the same interests, such as music, physical activity, sports, and socializing.

Unfortunately, that was then and this is now. Their respective visions for the relationship changed significantly with the addition of such aspects as financial responsibilities, managing a home and raising children, building a career, and perhaps even moving to a new suburb or city. Just because two people shared the same goals at an earlier stage of life, does not guarantee they will continue to want the same things for the rest of their lives. This is the reality of life and has nothing to do with whether the relationship is a good one or not.

People change and forget to tell one another.

Lillian Hellman

EXPLORING SHARED VISION WITHOUT JUDGMENT

In the following exercises you will be invited to describe your ideal relationship. It's important that you be honest with yourself when declaring your vision. It is also important to avoid making judgments about the vision you have. There is no right or wrong vision for an ideal relationship. There are simply different visions.

It is important to become clear on your vision. There is no

benefit in minimizing or concealing your vision in an effort to better align with the anticipated vision of your partner's. Simply honor what you value now. In Week 6 you will have the opportunity to see how your vision aligns with that of your partner.

WHAT IF OUR VISIONS ARE DIFFERENT?

If you are experiencing difficulty in your relationship it might mean you and your partner hold different visions. It might also mean you and your partner share the same vision but lack the skill to create your ideal relationship. This is a much easier challenge to resolve than if two individuals have different visions.

A lack of sufficient overlap in your visions—and a reluctance by either to change—may indicate that the relationship has reached its natural conclusion. Is this cause for despair? Is it doom and gloom? No.

On the contrary, when two people want very different experiences, it does not serve either person to maintain the relationship. In our experience, when two people have different dreams, they have two options:

Firstly, they can acknowledge that their dreams are different and release each other to pursue their own paths. That is mature love and respect, no matter how sad or disappointing it might be.

Secondly, one partner could try to persuade the other to come onto their side. If the differences are not significant, altering one's dreams might be possible. But where the differences are significant, the result is often a tug-of-war.

This is counter to creating a healthy relationship. A healthy relationship requires that both individuals are freely moving in the same direction, <u>by their own choice</u>. Coercion or emotional blackmail is bound to end in failure.

We imagine a healthy relationship as being somewhat like a three-legged race that most of us participated in as young children. For those unfamiliar with this game, a three-legged race occurs when a person has one of their legs tied to the leg of a partner, thus creating three legs between them the two of them.

What becomes painfully clear is unless both individuals are committed to moving in the same direction in a co-ordinated way, they make little progress. In fact, they often trip and fall. Relationships are like three-legged races.

Both you and your partner must have the same goals and be committed to moving in the same direction if you're hoping to reach your destination.

If you do not like the relationship you have

with your husband or wife, and you would like it to be different,

that desire alone will not change your relationship.

That change begins with the intention to change it.

How it will change depends upon the intention that you set.

Gary Zukav: *Seat of the Soul*

THE MAGIC WAND

Below is your first exercise in helping you to identify your ideal relationship. In Ted's work with couples he often invites them to do an exercise he calls 'The Magic Wand'.

In this exercise he tells the couple that he has a magic wand, and will come to their home and wave his magic wand over them while they are sleeping. The result is their relationship will immediately become better! However, because they are asleep when he waves his magic wand, they don't know their relationship is now better. Ted asks the following questions:

> ✍ **When you wake the next morning, what will you notice?**

> ✍ **How will you know your relationship is better? What will you see, hear or do that would convince you your relationship has changed for the better?**

> ✍ **What might other people notice about the two of you?**

> ✍ **What will you do that is different?**

> ✍ **What will your partner do that is different?**

This exercise is a fun way to help couples identify the specific changes that will improve their relationship. Some examples of answers received are:

- *"All of the dirty clothes would be off the floor."*

- *"My partner would have his arms around me."*

- *"My wife would kiss me and say, 'Good morning, my love' "*

- *"I would slip out of bed quietly, make coffee and bring a cup for my wife."*

- *"I would start sharing my thoughts and feelings openly and honestly with my husband."*

- *"I would call my wife during the day and ask her how her day is going."*

- *"My husband would call me and ask if I needed anything before he came home."*

- *"I would greet my husband with a kiss when he got home."*

- *"I would openly express my joy."*

- *"I would share my feelings easily and my partner would honor them."*

- *"My husband would open the car door for me."*

SPECIFIC AND POSITIVE

To benefit from this exercise it is important that your answers are *specific and positive*. Make sure you identify behaviors. If you are uncertain of whether you have identified a behavior, ask yourself whether it is something you can see or hear. Behaviors are actions a video camera could record. It is also important that the behaviors are positive—behaviors you want in your relationship rather than behaviors you don't want. Remember the principle of focus.

Don't be surprised if you initially have difficulty identifying the behaviors of your ideal relationship. In our experience it's common for people to more easily identify what they don't want. Others have never thoughtfully asked themselves the question, *"What do I want?"*

Many of us have been raised with the belief that relationships are about giving to others. Consequently we haven't given ourselves permission to identify, much less ask for, what we want in a relationship.

Still others hold the belief that if their partner really loved them, they would know what they want. While this notion seems to be the stuff that romantic fantasies are made of, the expectation that our lovers should somehow magically 'know' creates heartache and frustration in a relationship.

In our experience with hundreds of couples, we've noticed most people are not very good at mind reading. If you want your partner to know something, you have to tell them.

PAUSE AND PONDER

Now is the time to do the Magic Wand exercise. Imagine we have taken Ted's magic wand and waved it over you and your partner while you are sleeping. When you awaken in the morning, what will you notice that tells you your relationship is better? Remember, your list must contain answers that are specific and positive.

      ✒ **What will be the first indication that your relationship is better?**

      ✒ **What will you see or hear which indicates to you your relationship has changed?**

      ✒ **What would other people notice about the two of you?**

🐟 **What would you be doing that is different?**

🐟 **What would your partner be doing that is different?**

🐟 **How would you feel?**

THE POWER OF OBSERVATION

Another strategy that can help you describe your ideal relationship, is to identify couples whose relationship you admire. Notice what they do and how they relate. What do they say and do with each other? What behaviors of theirs would you like to include in your relationship?

You might even have a one-on-one chat with a couple whose relationship you admire, and ask them directly what they do to make their relationship successful. Most people would be eager to share their 'secrets' of a successful relationship with you.

PAUSE AND PONDER

> ⤏ **What couple relationship do you admire?**

> ⤏ **What do they do that makes their relationship successful?**

✎ **What behaviors would I like to include in my own relationship?**

KEEP, STOP, START

Another simple exercise to help you identify your ideal relationship is, '*Keep, Stop, Start*'. In our experience, identifying what to keep, what to stop, and what to start are necessary actions when making any kind of change. To have a better relationship, consider:

- What are the good things that are happening in my relationship now that I want to <u>keep</u> doing?
- What are the unpleasant things that are happening in my relationship now that I want to <u>stop</u> doing?
- What are new things that I want to <u>start</u> doing to improve my relationship?

The following series of questions will help you identify what to *keep*, *stop*, and *start* in your relationship right now:

KEEP:

☞ **What is working well in my relationship now?**

☞ **What activities or behaviors do I want to keep or have more of?**

STOP:

☞ **What isn't working well in my relationship right now?**

🐟 **What would I like to stop, have less of, or change completely?**

START:

🐟 **What would I like to initiate, or have my partner initiate, to improve our relationship?**

🐟 **What new things might I or my partner start doing to make our relationship better?**

THE MAGIC OF ATTRACTION

Another method to gain clarity on what works for you is to reflect upon the time in your relationship when you felt a great deal of attraction to your partner. Read the following carefully, and write your answers as accurately as possible. Just let it flow; don't ponder too much on any point.

> ✍ **What attracted you to your partner at the start of your relationship? What did he/she do that you experienced as attractive or desirable?**

> ✍ **Do you still find this attractive? If not, why not?**

➴ What attracted your partner to you at the start of your relationship? What did you do that he/she experienced as attractive or desirable?

➴ Do the two of you do these things now? What has changed?

ACCEPTANCE AND CURIOSITY

As you complete these exercises it's important to maintain an attitude of acceptance and curiosity for what is happening in your relationship at this time. Being judgmental, critical, blaming, or playing the *would've/could've/should've* game, is not helpful.

It is through the process of accepting reality that you begin to change what is. You can only take action <u>now</u>, in the present moment, and only once you have identified and confronted the truth in all its nakedness.

Curiosity about your life and your relationship is also important. Curiosity means to mentally step back and witness your life and your relationship from a distance without judgment or blame. When you take the opportunity to 'notice' yourselves in this way, you are better able to clearly see where change is required.

If you notice yourself blaming or shaming yourself or your partner, please stop. The goal of these exercises is not about blaming or shaming; rather they are about claiming responsibility for your life.

Blaming and shaming evokes anger and resentment, neither of which contributes to constructive change. Anger and resentment often result from resisting what is.

By accepting what is and keeping your focus on the present rather than the past, you avoid getting stuck.

The pain we experience is a form of non-acceptance,

an unconscious resistance to what is.

Always say 'yes' to the present moment.

What could be more futile, more insane than to create

inner resistance to something that already is?

Eckhart Tolle

The Power of Now

A WORD ON JUDGMENT

Some of you might find the request to suspend judgment confusing. On the one hand we ask you to 'suspend judgment', and at the same time we invite you to identify what works in your relationship and what doesn't work. Isn't this judgment?

The challenge is the multiple meanings words have in the English language. When we ask you to suspend judgment we suggest you stop the labeling of something as right/wrong or good/ bad. This form of judgment, or more precisely 'value judgment', is destructive to building a better relationship. Instead we invite you to simply notice what works and what doesn't. Then, make the choice to do what works.

There is no need to label something as good/bad or right/ wrong. This coloring only causes you to become upset, angry and resentful. However, noticing what is and is not working is necessary to achieve success.

Judgment is the constant evaluation of things
as right or wrong, good or bad. When you are
constantly evaluating, classifying, labeling,
analyzing, you create turbulence.

Deepak Chopra

The goal this week is to ponder and clearly identify your ideal relationship. By the end of the week you will have a clearer understanding of your ideal relationship and thus, your ideal partner.

SETH'S LIST

After Seth's marriage ended, he made the decision to pause before moving into another relationship. His therapist advised him it was important to take time to grieve the loss of his first relationship before entering another.

Equally important was the need to understand what contributed to the ending of his first relationship. Seth decided he wanted to identify what had worked and what had not worked in his relationship so he would be better equipped to choose a suitable partner for his next relationship.

Seth took a number of months to generate a list of what he wanted in his next relationship. He used the wisdom gained from his twenty years of marriage to help him to identify what had worked for him and what hadn't.

This is what Seth identified:

✎ I want a mate who is:

- positive, happy, content, optimistic
- soft spoken, articulate
- affectionate, enjoys touch
- sexual, playful
- smiles easily and often
- curious, open
- spiritual
- even-tempered
- friendly
- financially responsible
- has grown children
- non-smoker
- non-drinker
- non-drug user
- peaceful
- appreciative, readily expresses gratitude
- takes responsibility for their emotions

✎ My Ideal Relationship will:

- be peaceful, joyful, playful
- be sexual, and she will initiate sex as often as I do
- have shared decision making
- give each other space for self, family, couple, extended family, friendships, and community
- have shared parenting
- have open and honest communication
- respect and encourage change and growth
- be emotionally, physically, and psychologically safe
- be respectful, trusting
- be considerate and caring
- be balanced
- respect our private space and time
- be stable, grounded, centered
- be close but not attached
- be interdependent, not dependent
- accept each other's individuality
- be supportive

In completing his list, Seth developed a better understanding of his ideal relationship. Completing the list made it possible for Seth to identify someone who would have a high degree of overlap with his ideal relationship.

NON-NEGOTIABLE LIST

In addition to identifying what you want in your ideal relationship, it is important to identify preferences that we call 'non-negotiables'. In considering your ideal mate, some of your preferences will be relatively 'minor', while others will be 'major' preferences that are essential to creating your ideal relationship.

These 'minor' preferences are the negotiable items on your list. That is, while you may prefer them, they are not essential. Color of hair, eyes, height, weight and age may be examples of insignificant preferences. However, there will or ought to be aspects of your ideal relationship that are non-negotiable. That is, they must be present for you to experience a happy and healthy relationship.

If you want to experience a joyful and satisfying relationship it is vital that you are clear about those aspects of your relationship that are non-negotiable. In being clear on what is required for your relationship to work, you are able to decide whether someone is a good fit for you.

SUGGESTIONS FOR CREATING YOUR NON-NEGOTIABLE LIST

Separate the expectations and wishes of others (parents, society, friends) from your own wishes. This is your relationship. You are the one who needs to live in it.

Consider the kind of relationship that best fits with your personality, values, and goals in life, now and in the foreseeable future. Your non-negotiable list is not intended to be 'cast in stone'.

Rather it is a picture of where you are today. You can and should modify your list as you grow and have new experiences in life.

Be specific. General terms such as intimacy, mutual respect, freedom, affirmation, or feeling loved need to be defined more specifically. Distinguish clearly between what is negotiable and non-negotiable.

The following are suggested categories to consider for your list:

- Career
- Financial
- Education
- Communication Style
- Relationship Style
- Emotional Style
- Lifestyle
- Physical
- Interests, Leisure and Hobbies
- Sexuality
- Relationship Goals
- Spirituality
- Parenting Style
- Cultural Background
- Ethics and Values

- Religious Background
- Race and Ethnic Culture
- (Add as many others as you like)

LEANNE'S NON-NEGOTIABLE LIST

Leanne took time to create her list of negotiable and non-negotiable qualities. The following is her non-negotiable list for her ideal relationship:

⋙ Career

- Holds at least a college degree
- Has a professional/semiprofessional career
- Holds a steady job and has a regular income
- Understands success means more than making money
- Can make less money than I do but is financially self sufficient
- Has a job he finds meaningful and enjoys

⋙ Communication Style

- Can discuss most difficult or sensitive issues without becoming critical or defensive
- Vulnerable issues are respected and don't come back to be used against me

- Keeps an open mind on all issues; flexible rather than dogmatic

❧ Emotional Style

- Encouraging
- Can identify and express his emotions
- Is introspective
- Is open and transparent
- Peaceful, calm, soft-spoken

❧ Family, Friends, and Pets

- Has a good relationship with his mother and father
- Connected to his siblings and extended family
- Has a close relationship with his children
- Wants to have at least one more child with me
- Enjoys cats

❧ Financial Style

- Lives within his means
- Saves part of his salary
- Conservative with investments
- Pays off credit card balance monthly
- Doesn't gamble

⋙ Health

- Non smoker
- Social drinker
- Exercises regularly
- Eats healthily
- Has moderate to high energy level

⋙ Interests and Leisure Time

- Values being active
- Reads for personal growth
- Knows how to enjoy himself; can be alone

⋙ Relationship Style

- Views women in a positive light
- Is committed to our relationship
- Interested in being my friend as well as lover
- Is committed to a monogamous relationship

⋙ Sexual Style

- Enjoys playful sexuality
- Is sensitive and affectionate as well as sexual
- Tells me he cares in words and actions
- Accepts my body as it is

⋙ Spiritual

- Has a belief in a higher power
- Respectful of all forms of life
- Takes time to honor his spirituality
- Expresses gratitude for what he has in his life

YOUR OWN NON-NEGOTIABLE LIST

We invite you to make your non-negotiable list describing your ideal relationship. Forget your current relationship for now; focus only on what is ideal for you. Be completely honest with yourself. Make sure these are all clearly non-negotiable.

Career and education

Financial

Communication style

⤳ **Relationship style**

⤳ **Emotional style**

⤳ **Lifestyle / Physical / Health**

101 ☯

❧ **Interests, Leisure and Hobbies**

❧ **Sexuality**

❧ **Family, Friends, Pets**

Spirituality

Other:

CREATING A COLLAGE OR VISION BOARD

Another way of identifying your ideal relationship is to create a 'collage'. A collage is a compilation of pictures and words assembled on a poster board that represents your image of an ideal relationship. Some people also call this a 'Vision Board'.

Look through old magazines for pictures, images or words that capture the essence of your ideal relationship. Cut out the pictures, words or images and glue them on a large sheet of paper or poster board. Feel free to add or draw your own words or images.

People who are visual learners may find this an easier way to identify their ideal relationship.

A great online resource for doing this is *Pinterest*[3], a content sharing service that allows members to 'pin' images, videos and other objects to their pinboard.

Other methods that might work for you include writing poetry, painting a picture, sculpting or any other means of expressing your ideal relationship. Be creative. You might use aspects of favorite songs like Billy Joel's *Just the Way You Are* or a movie like *Avatar* as part of your montage of an ideal relationship.

HAVING THE TOOLS IN YOUR COMMUNICATION SKILLS TOOLBOX

In a few weeks you'll be asked to share the above description of your ideal relationship with your partner. However, before we ask you to do this, we believe it is essential that both you and your partner have the communication skills required to ensure a positive and successful sharing of information.

---

3   http://pinterest.com/

Over the next two weeks our focus will be on developing those communication skills to ensure you and your partner have adequate tools in your personal 'toolbox' to effectively communicate your vision of your ideal relationship. Our goal is for you to truly hear and understand each other's vision in an open and accepting way, and then respond in ways that support the process of relationship building.

SUMMARY

In Week 2 our intention has been to identify your ideal relationship. This is an essential step in creating a better relationship. By completing the exercises included in the chapter you should now have a clearer understanding of what your ideal relationship looks and feels like. This information can help you not only have a clearer picture of what your existing relationship looks like, but it will also help you create a better relationship for yourself.

While doing this exercise it is important to regularly ask yourself the question *"What do I want now?"* Stay open and honest with yourself. Listen carefully to what you have to say; to what your heart tells you. Armed with this information, you will be in a better position to create a relationship that works for you now and in the future.

In Week 3 you will learn some of the skills required to communicate effectively and respectfully with your partner.

PAUSE AND PONDER

➤ **What ideas stood out for you this week?**

➤ **What ideas were new for you?**

➤ **What ideas were challenging or difficult for you to accept or understand?**

➤ **What have you learned about yourself?**

What have you learned about your partner?

CONGRATULATIONS!

You have completed **Week 2** in your journey to a Better Relationship.

WEEK 3:

*Seek first to understand,
Then to be understood.*

Stephen Covey
The Seven Habits of Highly Effective People

WELCOME TO WEEK THREE.

Last week we explored the concept of knowing what you want, and also invited you to become clearer about what your ideal relationship would look and feel like. You were asked to identify the behaviors you desire in a relationship now. You were encouraged to be specific, concrete and positive.

Next, you were asked to identify those preferences that are negotiable and those that are non-negotiable. Finally, you were told that we would be inviting you to share your vision of your ideal relationship with your partner when we get to Week 6. To prepare you for that task, we will now address the vital aspect of effective and authentic communication.

COMMUNICATING EFFECTIVELY AND AUTHENTICALLY

This week we will share with you some of the skills required to communicate effectively with your partner. Our goal is to increase your ability to communicate your innermost thoughts and feelings clearly and confidently. You will learn:

- Communication is a skill
- The importance of understanding
- There are no mistakes
- Listening skills
- Making 'I' statements
- Telling your truth

COMMUNICATION IS A SKILL

An inability to communicate effectively is one of the most common reasons why relationships fail. And yet, communication is a skill, pure and simple. Effective communication can be learned.

Without doubt, some people are more skilled in their ability to communicate, while others are less skilled. Our goal in Week 3 is to increase your skill as a communicator.

In our work with couples we use the metaphor of a 'toolbox'. We all have a personal toolbox. Some people have many tools in their box, while others have a toolbox that is mostly empty. And some have a toolbox filled with all the wrong tools.

If your toolbox is mostly empty, it may be through no fault of your own. It may be that you simply haven't had the opportunities needed to acquire more or better tools. The good news is that it's never too late to acquire new tools.

If you are blaming either yourself or your partner because of your inability to communicate effectively, please stop. Ineffective communication doesn't mean you are bad people. Rather, it simply means you are currently unskilled.

What is important is to identify the tools that may be missing from your toolbox and make a commitment to acquire these tools. A general rule is, the more tools in your toolbox, the more effective you will be in the various situations you'll encounter in your relationship and in life.

SEEK FIRST TO UNDERSTAND

At the beginning of this chapter we featured a quotation from Stephen Covey, author of the classic best-seller *The Seven Habits of Highly Effective People*.

Covey believes one of the habits of successful people is they

"Seek first to understand, then to be understood".

We agree with Covey. The ability to understand one another is essential to a successful relationship. In our experience, a significant percentage of couples in conflict will say they don't understand their partner. Often they make statements such as, *"Boy, I just don't understand him!"* or, *"What's the matter with her?"* or, *"Wow, he's on a totally different planet!"*

The implied message is that there is something wrong with the other person.

In reality, such statements actually tell us more about the person making the statement. What is clear is this person doesn't understand his/her partner. Without understanding, partners in a relationship will constantly be 'at odds' with one another. In order to improve your relationship, you and your partner need to communicate in ways that make it possible for you to understand one another clearly and without judgment.

Notice that we're not asking if you agree with your partner, only <u>if you understand</u> your partner. This is an important distinction. Too often couples become stuck because they believe they must agree with one another. Not true! To have a better relationship, agreement is not necessarily required—however, understanding is.

The only people who listen to both sides of an argument are the neighbors.

Dave Abbott, Comedian

PAUSE AND PONDER

☞ When you and your partner struggle or argue, do you spend your time defending your position? Do you try to put yourself in your partner's shoes and sincerely listen and invest effort in trying to understand your partner's position? Do you listen in order to understand, or to win?

🐟 What do you do when you don't understand your partner?

🐟 What do you do when your partner doesn't understand you?

ALL BEHAVIOR MAKES SENSE

We believe all behavior makes sense. For this reason, no matter how ridiculous or irrational you might think someone else's behavior is, it's important to recognize that their behavior makes sense to them. No one says or does anything that doesn't make sense to them at the time! People behave as they do because their behavior is reasonable to them; in fact, it is the best solution they can access at that moment.

However, this isn't what our culture teaches us. Rather, in our culture we readily label some behaviors as 'mistakes'.

We want to challenge this notion of 'mistakes', and introduce the idea that a person's behavior is always the best tool they could find in their toolbox at that time to deal with a situation before them. In truth, we believe there are no such things as mistakes.

THERE ARE NO MISTAKES

The notion that there are no mistakes may be difficult for you to even consider. Most of us have been raised in a culture that unquestionably accepts the idea of 'mistakes', and the word is commonly found in our daily language. Speak to virtually everyone and they'll probably say they have made many mistakes in their life.

In our experience, some continually blame themselves for their past mistakes and as a result experience considerable shame and guilt. These people are some of our most frequent visitors wanting therapy.

During this week we invite you to consider a new way of looking at the events you have labeled 'mistakes'. Instead, we suggest you consider that what you have called a *mistake* was in fact the best decision available <u>at that moment</u>.

PAUSE AND PONDER

✎➳ **Think of a time when you made a 'mistake'. List some of your 'mistakes' below.**

✎➳ **With respect to each 'mistake' that you listed above, answer the following questions:**

> 1. **Did you know your action was a mistake at the time you made your decision?**

2. At what point did you decide your action was a mistake?

3. What did you think about this action at the time you made the decision?

4. What were the factors that led you to choose the action you did?

20/20 HINDSIGHT

In completing the exercise above, you probably quickly recognized that at the time you chose the action you now call a 'mistake', you didn't think it *was* a mistake. Think about it: if you did, you certainly wouldn't have taken that action! You made the choice you made because you thought it was the right action or solution at the time.

It was probably only some time after the event that you experienced the *results* of your decision, and decided your choice or action was a 'mistake'.

The problem with labeling such decisions as 'mistakes' is that for most people, this label leads to feelings of shame, guilt, and fear of taking further actions in the future. This process is destructive.

When you call something a 'mistake' you discount the passage of time and the acquisition of more knowledge or skills that didn't exist at the time when you made your original decision.

Some time later, possibly even minutes or seconds later, you acquired additional information and insights, and with this additional information you might decide that you would have been better off making a different decision.

It's important to acknowledge that *you didn't have all this information at the time you made your original decision.*

No reasonable person would consciously decide, *"I'm going to make a mistake".* All of us choose the most reasonable and attractive alternative available to us at that moment. We might later have regretted a decision; however, it would not be accurate to say it was a mistake. At the time it was the best decision available.

LOSING MY VIRGINITY TO A COMPLETE IDIOT!

One of Ted's favorite stories comes from a workshop he participated in with Ray Woollam, author of *On Choosing With a Quiet Mind* and *Have a Plain Day.* In the workshop Woollam asked each participant to identify his or her biggest mistake. One young woman blurted out that her biggest mistake was '*losing her virginity to a complete idiot*'.

When the laughter died down, Woollam asked the young woman to recall the moment when she first had sexual relations. As the young woman recalled the memory, her face began to glow. She shared a wonderful story of a romantic evening that culminated in her making love.

Woollam then asked her, "*On this particular evening, did you like this man?*"

"*Yes!*" was her reply.

"*Did you find him attractive?*"

Her reply was an enthusiastic "*Yes!*".

"*Did you willingly consent to sleeping with this man?*"

"*Oh, yes!*"

"*So, when did you discover he was a 'complete idiot'?*"

"About six months later . . .", she replied.

"Ahhh", said Woollam, *"but at the time when you made the decision to sleep with him, you didn't know this. With the information and skills you possessed that evening, you decided he was a wonderful person to experience your first sexual intimacy with."*

"Yes!" she replied.

And she understood.

WHEN I PULL THE ARROW IN MY BOW...

According to Woollam, the concept of 'mistake' is not a universal concept. It does not exist in every culture in the world. Woollam tells the story of working with a group of young First Nations people who had become 'civilized' and separated from their traditional roots. He invited each of them to identify the biggest mistake of their life. Each had plenty of examples to offer.

Having heard their mistakes, Woollam then called a break in the workshop. During the interval he invited each of them to call an elder in their community who spoke their Native language. He requested they ask the elder for the exact word in their Native tongue for 'mistake'.

After they had all made their phone calls, the participants returned to the conference room. To everyone's surprise, not one person was able to provide a word for mistake in his or her native language. This is because the concept of 'mistake' simply doesn't exist in most aboriginal cultures.

The closest to our Western concept of mistake was a word that translated into the concept: "*When I pull the arrow in my bow, sometimes the arrow doesn't go where I intended.*" There was no blame or criticism attached to this word, only the observation that one doesn't always get the results one intends.

ALL TRYING OUR BEST

You might wonder why we have made such efforts to explain this concept to you. It's because we have come to know that all people invariably do the best they can with the tools they have available. Every person makes the best decision available at the time given his or her knowledge, skills, perspective, experience, and awareness of self and others.

If you are able to accept this idea, you are less likely to judge yourself or others too harshly. Instead, you are more likely to invest the time and energy needed to better understand how you and others think and perceive the world as you and they do.

It's been said that all conflict occurs between people or groups of people who each think they are right. If we apply this principle to couple relationships, it means that disagreements occur between two people who both think they are right. In our experience this is absolutely true. Each person from his/her own perspective believes they are right!

The problem is that we live in a world where we have a tendency to believe that if someone is right, then the other must be wrong. Could it be possible that there are two 'right' perspectives?

When we engage the world from the perspective that both could be 'right', we begin to address our differences using compassion and curiosity rather than conflict. *"I'm right, you're wrong"* is a form of war. Our goal this week is to increase your ability to understand your partner's perspective in an effort to increase your compassion and shared understanding.

THREE BLIND MEN AND AN ELEPHANT

There is an old fable about three blind men and an elephant. As the story goes, one of the men is standing near the front of the elephant. As he holds the elephant's trunk the first blind man says, *"This creature is long and thick and round. It must be a snake."*

The second blind man is standing at the side of the elephant and gets hold of one of its legs.

He exclaims, *"No, you're wrong. It's round and sturdy like a tree trunk. It must be a tree."*

The third blind man is positioned at the back of the elephant and is holding onto its tail.

"No, you're both wrong", he says. *"It's thin like a rope. It must be a rope."*

Of course each of the men is holding a different part of the elephant and though their descriptions are all different, they are all correct.

The problem is, because of their blindness, each has only

a limited view or understanding of the creature they have encountered. If they were to pool their information and resources, they would have a fuller perspective and just might understand what it is they have before them.

In life, all of us are blind to some degree. None of us has all the information all of the time. And like these blind men in our fable, we have a tendency to think our perspective is right and the other's perspective is wrong.

This kind of thinking keeps us stuck and in conflict with one another.

When we accept that each person's perspective is valid and makes sense to them we open up to the possibility of discovering something larger than our own experience. In any situation where we disagree with another it may be that we are simply 'holding on to a different part of the elephant'.

Many couples that find themselves in conflict are like these three blind men. Each is telling their truth from their perspective. While accurate, they fail to take into consideration that the other is also telling the truth from their perspective.

Anyone reading this book will have had plenty of experience where they and their partner had different perspectives of some past event. Sadly, many couples stay stuck because they refuse to accept the possibility that both might be right!

Life is like an elephant. It is larger and more complex than most of us acknowledge.

PAUSE AND PONDER

✍ **Think of a time when you and your partner disagreed, only to later discover that both of you were 'right' from your own perspectives. Describe this experience below.**

✍ **How did you feel when you discovered an even larger 'truth' existed that incorporated both of your individual truths?**

ZACH AND HELENA

Zach and Helena had been struggling in their relationship for a number of years. Their struggles became more apparent after their eldest daughter Sarah turned fourteen. Each parent had a different idea of how best to parent Sarah. Zach thought Helena was too soft and was making Sarah into an irresponsible adolescent. Helena thought Zach was too hard and feared he would push Sarah to leave home early.

When it came to setting consequences for Sarah's misdeeds, Zach and Helena frequently argued until one of them became exhausted and gave in. Not surprisingly, it was common for each of them to feel angry and discounted by the actions of the other.

A counselor invited Zach and Helena to make a list of the qualities they desired in their daughter. Zach's list included qualities such as honesty, responsibility, conscientious, hard working, and punctual. Helena's list included qualities such as happy, peaceful, content, friendly and outgoing.

The counselor then asked Zach and Helena to combine their lists on one page and invited them to consider consequences that honored all of the qualities and not just some of them.

This process helped Zach and Helena to accept each other's values and to look for ways to support the other's values as well as their own. When Zach and Helena stopped playing, *"I'm right, you're wrong"* and instead started playing, *"We're both right"*, they got along much better and were more effective in parenting Sarah.

HONOR ALL PERSPECTIVES

In any relationship it is important to recognize that both individuals hold 'truths' or perspectives that are valid. Each partner must give recognition to and honor the other's perspective as well as their own. Discussions that end in argument usually occur because one or both individuals believe they are right and the other person is wrong. They think that only one person can be right at a time.

If you believe that only one of you can be right, then any disagreement will end with one of you winning and the other losing. In our experience, a system that creates a loser can never lead to harmony. We encourage you to consider the possibility that <u>both</u> of you can be right even when you disagree with one another.

If you create winners and losers in your relationship,

the winner will always be living with a loser

and his/her resentment.

ACTIVE LISTENING

All understanding starts with listening. But the truth is, most people are not good listeners. They are more intent on telling others what they think, and less interested in hearing what others think. Listening requires that we keep our mouth closed and our ears open. We also need to have an open mind and an open heart.

125

It is not uncommon for people in a long-term relationship to assume they already know what their partner is going to say or do. They claim they have heard it all before, and think there is nothing new to hear or learn. They forget that their partner is constantly evolving and changing and is a different person today than he or she was yesterday.

Another common challenge is one partner assumes he or she knows better. They assume their opinion is more informed or more valid than their partner's. They think they have more experience, education or some other quality that qualifies them to being 'right'.

This is a recipe for disaster. Can you see how this attitude of 'superiority' blocks one partner from hearing the other's point of view, and acts as a barrier to new information?

It is said we can only learn when we are prepared to admit we don't know something. How true.

THE ZEN MASTER

There is a Zen story that captures the wisdom of being open to new ideas. In the story, a young monk visits his Master and asks the Master to share his wisdom. The Master first invites the young monk to have tea with him. The Master pours tea into the young monk's cup but fails to stop pouring when the cup is full.

The young monk is startled by this and says, "*Master, what are you doing? Why are you pouring the tea all over the floor?*"

The Master replies, "*There isn't enough room in your cup.*"

The point the Master is making is that unless the young monk is open and receptive to new ideas, there will be no space to put new information in.

Many of us are like the young monk. We are so full of our own ideas that we have no room to hear the wisdom of others.

Until we make space for new ideas to come in, these ideas will elude us.

PAUSE AND PONDER

How effective a listener are you? Here are questions to help you to assess your effectiveness as a listener.

> One way to determine if you are a good a listener is to ask those around you. Ask your partner, children, and co-workers if they feel 'heard' when they tell you something. Are there topics you hear better than others?

> Notice whether people tend to repeat themselves when conversing with you. People will often repeat themselves when they don't feel heard.

> Do people raise their voices when communicating with you? People will often raise their voice when they don't feel heard.

✍ Do people seek you out and tell you things about themselves or do people withhold information from you? If people seek you out it's a good indication that people find you a good listener.

✍ When in conversation with others, who is doing most of the talking? Is there a healthy balance between talking and listening, or is the listening one-sided?

✍ Do you find yourself interrupting with a comment, an opinion or a story of your own before the other person has finished their sentence or story?

✍ When you are in a conversation do you keep focused on the other person's face, eyes and gestures, or are you constantly looking around and engaged in some activity of your own?

✍ Would you seek out someone like yourself to share something important? This is probably the best test of whether you are a good listener.

HAVE I GOT IT RIGHT?

The following is an excellent exercise to help you improve your effectiveness as a listener. Have a conversation with another person. Allow them to speak first. After they have spoken for a few minutes, ask them to stop.

Then share with them what you thought you heard them say. Simply reflect back what you heard.

You are not to respond to their questions or add your own thoughts. Your only task is to 'mirror' back what you thought you heard. Once you've done this, ask *"Have I got it right?"*

Allow the other person to tell you what you got and what you missed. You may find you need to make a number of attempts before you accurately and completely reflect back all that was said.

When you have accurately reflected what the other said, invite them to tell you more. You do this by asking, *"Is there anything else?"* Follow this process until the other person has said all they wish to say.

The process sounds like this:

> *"Share something with me."*
>
> *"What I heard you say is . . . ."*
>
> *"Have I got it right?"*
>
> *"Is there anything else?"*

The first thing you will notice when doing this exercise, is that the conversation is <u>focused solely on listening</u>. It isn't about who's right or who's wrong. It isn't about telling your side of a story. It isn't even about solving a problem. It is solely about listening to what the other is communicating to you.

Once you have completed this exercise, ask the other person what it was like for them. Most people will report how unusual it was to be listened to so completely. Common replies are that they felt *heard, close to you, uplifted, honored* and *respected.* Amazing, isn't it?

This is a rich and inspiring experience for most people. You'll discover that you understand the other person even more. This skill is especially useful when having a disagreement with someone and you don't understand his or her perspective. You can easily move to a place of greater understanding simply by listening more effectively.

TIPS FOR MORE EFFECTIVE LISTENING

The following is a list of suggestions to help you to listen more effectively. How many of them do you practice?

- Stop talking.

- Lean forward and get close to the other person.

- Sit down and invite the other person to sit down too. Look the person in the eye.

- Notice their facial expressions.

- Make a conscious intention to understand. Forget about agreeing or disagreeing. Let go of problem solving or telling your side of the story.

- Get rid of distractions. Turn off the television, radio, phones or other distractions.

- Concentrate fully on the person. Make it a goal to understand the person and not just hear their verbal message.

- Listen for the most important points.

- Be patient.

- Be present.

- Keep acknowledging and probing until the speaker lets you know he or she has finished telling you everything they wish to share.

- Keep your mind receptive and open.

- Ask questions for clarification.

- Let go of 'win-lose' and 'right-wrong'. Remember, the other person's point of view is as valid as your own.

- Let go of what your response will be.

- Take as much time as needed to listen fully.

If you listen with the intention of understanding the other's point of view, you'll discover your ability to communicate with your partner will improve by this change alone. Give your partner 'permission' to inform you when he or she doesn't feel heard.

They might do this by a simple statement like, "*It feels like you're not hearing what I'm saying right now.*" This is a helpful way of informing you when you may not be listening effectively.

'I' MESSAGES VS 'YOU' MESSAGES

A second and very powerful tool necessary for effective communication is the use of 'I' messages. An 'I' message is simply that—a statement that shares information about you with others; about what you are thinking and feeling.

'I' messages are always true statements because they are statements you make about yourself. And because they are true statements, they can't be argued with. The following are examples of 'I' messages:

- I'm tired.
- I feel scared when you drive so close to the other cars.
- I'm concerned we won't have enough money to pay our rent this month.
- I'm not in the mood for love making tonight.
- I'm feeling close to you right now.
- I'm really enjoying being with you right now.
- I don't understand what you just said.

- I'm frustrated with my inability to be understood by you.

- I'm feeling misunderstood.

- I love you.

- I'm sad.

- I like your idea.

- I'm feeling very vulnerable right now.

When couples are in conflict, often it's because one or both are making 'you' messages rather than 'I' messages. A 'you' message is a statement about the other person. These statements typically begin with the word 'you', though not always.

Because the statement is about the other person, it is open to disagreement. With a 'you' message, you are declaring who the other person is or is not. It is therefore not surprising that a 'you' statement often results in disagreement or even conflict.

Frequently, 'you' messages have an accusing tone and contain blame and judgment. Examples of 'you' messages are:

- You don't love me anymore.

- You don't do enough around the house.

- You are lazy and inconsiderate.

- You never do the dishes.

- You're wrong.

- You are happy.

- You spend too much money.
- You never put the cap on the toothpaste.
- You are wonderful.
- You didn't try hard enough.
- You never put down the toilet seat.
- You don't spend enough time with me.
- You watch too much TV.
- You're always on the phone to your friends.
- You don't love me like you used to.
- You drink too much.

Can you feel the difference between the 'you' messages and the 'I' messages listed above? How does it feel to receive an 'I' message? How does it feel to receive a 'you' message? How does it feel to give an 'I' message? How does it feel to give a 'you' message?

What you might notice is that 'I' messages are an act of intimacy. They reveal information about you to another. They disclose information about what you are thinking and/or feeling.

'You' messages, on the other hand, tend to be confrontational because they are declarations you make about the other person.

'You' messages frequently contain elements of accusation or blame or judgment. Because they are statements about others, they are open to disagreement.

'You' messages share nothing about you and contribute

to creating disagreement rather than intimacy. If you want to improve the effectiveness of your communication, commit to using 'I' messages as often as possible. Tell your truth about who you are and invite your partner to tell their truth about who they are.

If both partners are using 'I' messages, the possibility of a shared understanding increases significantly.

Even if only one partner in the relationship makes a commitment to using 'I' messages, the effectiveness of the conversations will change significantly.

PAUSE AND PONDER

      ❦ **Practice using 'I' messages. Write out a number of statements describing what you think and how you feel. Make sure each of these statements begins with the word 'I' and are statements solely about you.**

➳ **Try sharing your 'I' messages with others and notice the difference in your relationships.**

TELLING YOUR TRUTH

One of the keys to a better relationship is your willingness and ability to tell your truth about you. Truth telling is not just about honesty or dishonesty. Rather, telling the truth is about *revealing* who you are. To create an intimate relationship it is necessary you tell your partner *who you are deeply and intimately.*

Humans are very complex beings, and we have many thoughts and feelings at the same time. Often we are not fully conscious of all we think and feel.

Also, our level of awareness and consciousness changes and grows continuously throughout our life. As we come to know ourselves better, we need to continually inform our partner about who we are. We need to keep them up to date about who we are now.

We also change and grow throughout our lives. Who we are at age forty is very different than who we were at age twenty. As our thoughts, beliefs, values and perspectives change, we must continually inform our partner about who we are if we want to stay connected. We must continually reveal our inner truth. We must let others know who we are in this moment.

If we don't continually reveal who we are, how can we expect others to understand or recognize us? And how can we expect to understand our partner and grow with them if we don't allow space for them to reveal who they?

Telling your truth is how the two of you will remain intimate.

SUMMARY

Communicating effectively is vital to growing a better relationship. By listening more actively and by telling the truth from your perspective using 'I' messages, your connection and compassion with one another deepens. And while there are many more skills involved in effective communication, these are two of the most basic and most important. Practice them until you become highly skilled in their use.

PAUSE AND PONDER

 ❧ **What ideas stood out the most for you this week?**

➥ **What ideas were new for you?**

➥ **What ideas were challenging and difficult for you to accept or understand?**

➥ **What did you learn about yourself?**

➥ **What did you learn about your partner?**

CONGRATULATIONS!

You have completed **Week 3** on your journey to a Better Relationship.

～WEEK 4:

We cannot know ourselves in isolation.
We can only know ourselves
in relationship.

Neale Donald Walsch

WELCOME TO WEEK FOUR.

Last week we discussed the importance of creating a foundation of a shared understanding with your partner.

We explored the concept of 'mistake' and introduced the idea that all people choose the best option available to them at each moment.

We explained the difference between 'I' messages and 'You'

messages, and the significance of revealing the truth about yourself if you wish to create intimacy in your relationship.

This week our focus is on how to resolve differences when they occur in your relationship. In our discussions we will address the following:

- The blessing of relationships

- Respecting differences

- Resolving differences successfully

- Emotional boundaries

- Relationship styles

THE BLESSING OF RELATIONSHIPS

Relationships are a wonderful gift! They provide us with opportunities to experience joy, happiness and intimacy in life.

Relationships, however, are more than simply an opportunity to 'feel good'. A relationship is the primary means to *discover who you are.*

You cannot know yourself in isolation. You can only know yourself through a relationship. You can only know who you are relative to other people and events.

Because of this, relationships are sacred spaces. It is through your relationships with others that you are given opportunities to experience yourself as loving, kind, generous, forgiving, patient and understanding, among other qualities. It is impossible to know these qualities about yourself in isolation. This is one of the reasons to be grateful for the relationships you now enjoy.

I've come to see that to be fully human
we need other people.

Individual growth
is intimately linked with relationships.

Hugh Prather

BEING GRATEFUL FOR THE CHALLENGES TOO

It is easy to be grateful for your relationship when it is joyful, exciting and loving. It is more difficult to be grateful when your relationship is challenging or going through tough times. Yet, it is through these challenges that the greatest opportunities exist to grow and evolve as a human being.

(It may be helpful for you to recall our discussion in Week 1 of seeing a crisis as an opportunity.)

The challenges we encounter in relationship are indicators of a need for further growth; an indication that further mastery of skills and the need to expand and deepen our understanding of our self, others, and of the world is required. Our sufferings, disappointments and hardships have the potential to be our greatest teachers.

The Buddha stated: "*Even loss and betrayal can bring us awakening*". He invited us to, "*Imagine every person in the world is enlightened. They are all your teachers, each doing just the right things to help you learn perfect patience, perfect wisdom, and perfect compassion.*"

Below is a beautiful poem that speaks to the gifts that are available in our challenges and suffering.

Native Blessing

Bless these our circumstances.
Bless the hardship and the pain.
Bless the hunger and the thirst.
Bless the locusts and the drought.
Bless the things which do not turn out right.
Bless those who take all and give not.
In these circumstances, find growth.
In growth, discover clarity.
In clarity, an inner vision.

Nancy Wood

Does this mean we should seek out misfortune and difficult circumstances because that's the best way to grow? Some people believe that's absolutely true; that tough times are our greatest opportunity for optimum spiritual advancement.

According to therapist Stephanie Marston, "... *the word* crisis *means 'a separating', or 'a turning point.' So, by realizing that part of us has to die so that the rest of us can come to life, we can emerge as a new, reborn person.*"

And while it feels logical and natural to want to escape our crisis or discomfort as quickly as possible, it is in fact this very discomfort which initiates and accelerates growth at a deep level.

When the discomfort becomes acute, we are motivated to take action. And so, ironically, pain is necessary—even essential—to our growth. Instead of running from pain or being in denial about it, confront the pain and embrace it as an agent of change. American Buddhist nun and author Pema Chödrön supports this. She says, "*...whatever life you're in is a vehicle for waking up pain.*"

We have begun this week with these thoughts in the hope you will look at the challenges in your relationship in a new way. It is our wish that you let go of seeing challenge as something to be avoided, and begin to see that your struggles are opportunities to grow and evolve as a human being... and to grow in your relationship.

When we expect benefits from our challenges, we have the potential to use these experiences as powerful tools in the development of self knowledge.

These experiences are opportunities for more intimacy in our relationships. When we look for the blessings in our struggles, we begin to see beyond the darkness of the struggle. We begin to discover the benefits of seeing the glass as 'half full'.

IT'S ALL ABOUT ATTITUDE

When something challenging happens, how do you respond? Do you become angry, resentful and bitter? Do you feel and act as if you have been victimized and retreat into a 'poor me' posture? Or do you look upon the event as a gift that has the potential to teach you a valuable lesson in life?

The next time something in your life goes 'wrong', consider setting aside your anger and disappointment for just a moment. Instead, ask yourself the questions: *"How might this experience benefit me?"* *"What could this experience offer me?"* *"How might I use this event to become stronger, more patient, or a better person?"* *"What wisdom might I acquire through this experience?"*

No matter how dismal your circumstances or how bad your experience may be, you always have choice as to how you respond to the circumstances in your life.

And you can change you attitude in an instant. It's entirely in your hands—or rather, your mind.

Psychologist Viktor Frankl, author of *Man's Search For Meaning*, shared his experience of being in the concentration camp in World War II. He considers the ability to choose how we respond as *"the last of the human freedoms"*.

Author Troy Chapman believes that *"the freedom to respond may be the only total freedom we have"*.

Many people believe that life happens <u>to</u> them; that they have little or no choice. But of course this isn't true: while we often have no choice about the *events* that occur in our life, we <u>always</u> have a choice in the *meaning* we give to these events.

Depending on the meaning we assign, we can have an entirely different experience of the same event.

Here's a simple example. Rowan goes golfing for the afternoon and shoots a score of 78. If Rowan is a highly skilled golfer he might be really disappointed with his score. However, if Rowan is a novice, a score of 78 might be a dream come true for him.

Do you see how it isn't the score that determines Rowan's experience of his afternoon of golf? Rather it's *the meaning Rowan assigns to his score.*

Our experience of life is created in following way:

Event ➜ Meaning ➜ Experience

We all have events that occur in life. Yet the *experience* we have is not dependent upon those events, but on the *meaning* we assign to the event.

Here's another example. A woman in labor delivering a baby is in significant pain. But because she knows she is delivering her child, she experiences joy even while she is in pain. The pain doesn't have to mean suffering. It isn't the pain that determines her experience, rather it's the meaning she assigns to the pain.

It's incredible what a difference a simple change in meaning can make. While it's impossible to change an event that has already occurred, you can change the meaning you give to the event. In an instant, at any time. By changing the meaning, you can change your experience of a past event.

> *We are not disturbed by what happens to us,*
> *but by our thoughts about what happens to us.*

Epictetus : Greek Philosopher

Notice that this also has profound implications on current and future events. All too often people focus attention and energy on complaining about something they're involved in, or something that is coming up.

A more effective use of their energy would be in changing the meaning they assign to the event. This is what we are doing when we rename a challenging situation as an 'opportunity'.

By assigning a different meaning we *change our perspective*, and are able to have a different experience of the same situation or event. In turn, this can result in a very different response.

In his book *Peace Begins With Me*, Ted tells the very moving and highly personal story of how a sudden epiphany turned years of frustration, self-pity, anger and resentment about his disabled son into a wonderful blessing and an opportunity for growth. The title says it all.

Remember the quotation we shared with you in Week 1—if

you continue to do more of the same, you'll continue to get the same results. If you want to have a new experience in life, you must do something *different than you've done before*. When you change your meaning, you change your experience of an event.

BELIEFS ABOUT DISAGREEMENT

Following on from the above, it will be clear that the meaning you give to disagreements in your relationship affects the way you respond to the disagreements when they occur... and also how you remember them.

The meaning you assign affects your ability to see the opportunities available in your struggles. This principle is equally true of the disagreements you encounter in your relationships.

PAUSE AND PONDER

Consider the following statements. Circle those that reflect the beliefs you currently hold about disagreement in relationships.

A. Disagreement is an indication that two people aren't meant to be together.

B. Disagreement is a normal part of everyday life because people perceive and experience the world in different ways.

A.   Disagreement is always a negative experience.

B.   Disagreement can be a positive or negative experience depending upon our skill and ability to resolve disagreements successfully.

A.   Disagreements create distance between people.

B.   Disagreements can create more intimacy between people because they create an opportunity to know someone more fully .

A.   Disagreements always weaken relationships.

B.   Disagreements can strengthen relationships.

A.   Disagreements should be avoided at all costs.

B.   Disagreements can be a catalyst for increasing awareness of our self and our connections with others.

SCORING:

If you identified primarily with the perspective expressed in the 'A' statements, then disagreements have the potential to destroy your relationship. You fear disagreement and do not appreciate the benefits it offers.

If you identified primarily with the perspectives expressed in the 'B' statements, you recognize that disagreement can be an opportunity to create more honesty and intimacy in your relationship. You recognize that disagreement can present an opportunity to grow and evolve into a human being who can celebrate and honor the differences between people rather than be negatively affected by their differences.

Many couples with relationship difficulties perceive any form of disagreement as negative, and to be avoided at all costs. This perception may be due to the perspectives they learned from childhood. It may also be the result of having inadequate tools in their toolbox to successfully resolve differences in their relationships.

If you do not know how to resolve differences effectively and respectfully, then any difference can pose a threat to the health and longevity of your relationship. The following suggestions will assist you in resolving differences and disagreements more successfully.

SUGGESTIONS FOR RESOLVING DISAGREEMENTS SUCCESSFULLY

1. Consider the possibility that disagreements are acceptable—even helpful.

2. Accept all points of view as legitimate and valid. Suspend right/wrong, good/bad thinking. Let go of the need to be right.

3. Be open to change. Be willing to allow your (and your partner's) thoughts, ideas and values to evolve and change over time.

4. Be willing to be influenced by the legitimate point of view of others.

5. Take 100% responsibility for your emotional responses. Remember that while you have little or no control over what happens to you, you have total control over _how you respond_ to what happens to you.

6. Utilize active listening skills. Identify and clarify what the other person is thinking and feeling. Confirm that you understand what they are saying before responding.

7. Speak your truth openly. Share your thoughts and feelings. Use 'I' messages to reveal what you are thinking and feeling.

8. Utilize collaboration skills to create win-win solutions.

9. Be thankful for the opportunities differences have offered.

10. Trust in a higher order to the universe. Trust that disagreements occur in life to create exactly the right opportunities to learn and grow.

DISAGREEMENTS REVEAL DIFFERENT TRUTHS

It's impossible for couples not to experience disagreement at some time in their relationship.

People come from varied and diverse backgrounds. We all have different experiences in the world, and we have been taught different beliefs about how the world is. At some point these differences will show themselves.

If we engage the world from a purely right/wrong perspective, like the three blind men in Week 3, then our differences can make life very difficult. However, if we engage the world from the perspective that each individual is telling their truth as they know it, then differences can enlighten us.

Differences can help us to learn and experience truths we haven't yet come to know.

Whenever you experience disagreement in your relationship, it is because your partner has a perspective that is different from yours.

He/she wants something different than you want, or they perceive the world differently from how you perceive it.

Later in the book, during Week 5, you will be guided through a number of exercises to help you to recognize how you and your partner see and experience the world differently.

But for now, we will add some skills for successfully resolving differences to your personal toolbox.

THE FIVE STYLES OF RESOLVING DIFFERENCES

There are many ways of resolving differences; however, we have found the matrix on the opposite page to be very useful.

It suggests five different styles for resolving differences. Being competent in each of these is like having five different tools in your toolbox.

The particular tool or style you use depends upon two factors:

- The importance of achieving your goal
- The importance of maintaining your relationship

The five styles for resolving differences are:

1. **Competing**

2. **Avoiding**

3. **Accommodating**

4. **Compromising**

5. **Collaborating**

In the diagram on the top of the next page, each of these styles is positioned relative to the importance of Achieving your Goal, and the importance of Maintaining the Relationship.

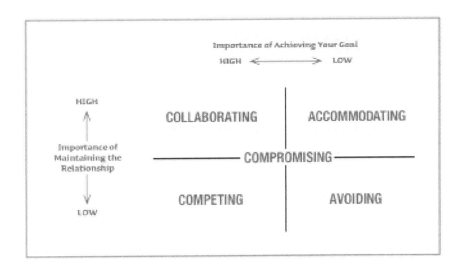

For example, if you have a high desire to achieve your own goals, and a low desire to maintain the relationship, the style will be *Competing*. (Each is discussed in detail further below).

Each style of resolving differences has its place. What you need to decide is whether the style you are using is working for you with regard to a specific situation. To be truly effective in resolving challenges, you need to be skilled in all five strategies and be prepared to vary your resolution style according to the circumstances and individuals involved.

Or, in other words, you need to select the right tool for the job. The more tools in your personal toolbox, the more likely you will be successful in accomplishing your desired outcome.

Skills for resolving differences are not something you are born with. These skills are learned.

The following is a detailed description of the five styles of resolving differences. Read through the various styles and as you do, consider the following questions:

- What style do you use most often?

- What is the outcome of using this particular style?

- Is your typical style of resolving differences working for you?

- Which style(s) do you need to add to your toolbox?

1. COMPETING

When Indicated:

Importance of Achieving Your Goal:	High
Importance of Maintaining the Relationship:	Low

The Competing style of resolution is typically characterized by aggressive and uncooperative behaviors. The individual pursues his/her own concerns at the other's expense. It is a power-oriented style of resolution where the individual uses whatever power seems appropriate to win or to get his/her way.

A Competing style is commonly found in business or athletic situations. It is used when a person is highly ambitious and will stop at nothing to achieve their goal to get ahead.

A Competing style in a relationship occurs when one partner is dominant and dogmatic and is determined to get the outcome they desire. This style can also be referred to as controlling or manipulative.

Advantages:

The competing style is useful when there is insufficient time to create a better solution and a resolution is urgently required. It is often used in a formal hierarchy such as a business where achieving a goal is more important than maintaining the relationship. Clearly it is the style used in athletic competition or other relationship that are intended to identify winners and losers.

Disadvantages:

The competing style of resolution in a relationship breeds resentment and hostility toward the person using it. This style forces resolutions onto problems, which typically result in inadequate long-term solutions. *It is impossible to be truly intimate with someone who consistently competes because it does not feel safe to be in this kind of relationship.*

Long Term Result: Win - Lose

2. AVOIDING

When Indicated:

Importance of Achieving Your Goal:	Low
Importance of Maintaining Relationship:	Low

The Avoiding style of resolution is characterized by unassertive and uncooperative behaviors. The individual does not pursue his own concerns nor does he acknowledge the concerns of others. Rather, the person ignores challenges and avoids attempts to resolve them.

The Avoiding individual sidesteps issues, postpones decision-making, and/or withdraws. Like the ostrich with its head in the sand, he thinks the problem will go away if he simply ignores it.

Advantages:

The advantage of the Avoiding style of resolution is that it maintains the present status quo.

Avoiders resist change from occurring. In some situations it is not worth your time or effort to address a situation.

The goal is not that important to you and you have little desire to maintain a relationship. A phone call from a telephone solicitor might be a situation where avoiding works well for you.

Disadvantages:

The disadvantage of this style in a relationship is that challenges remain unresolved. The avoiding individual must live with the decisions of others. This can generate resentment and hostility over the long term. *It's impossible to be truly intimate with someone who avoids.* This is because avoiders do not reveal who they are.

Long Term Result: Lose - Lose

3. ACCOMMODATING

When Indicated:

Importance of Achieving Your Goal: Low

Importance of Maintaining Relationship: High

The Accommodating style of resolution is characterized by cooperative yet unassertive behaviors. The person neglects his own concerns in order to satisfy the concerns of the other.

This is a self-sacrificing style of resolution where the individual uses generosity, charity, obeying or yielding as the method of resolving the challenge. This is frequently found in a job situation where a worker needs to hold onto their job and so accommodates to the wishes of the manager. This style also occurs in a marriage where one partner thinks the best way to keep the peace is by doing whatever their partner wants. Accommodation requires the acceptance of the other's solution. One's own interests are not adequately addressed.

Advantages:

The accommodating style is useful when maintaining the relationship short term is more important than the achieving a goal. It also generates a quick solution when time is limited. It generates short-term peace.

Disadvantages:

The accommodating style of resolution tends to breed resentment and hostility in the long term, since the accommodating person eventually feels taken advantage of by others.

Similarly, the stronger partner often loses respect for the individual who always agrees and never says 'no'.

It is impossible to be intimate with someone who consistently accommodates, because they do not reveal who they are and what is important to them.

Long Term Result: Lose - Win

4. COMPROMISING

When Indicated:

Importance of Achieving Your Goal: Moderate

Importance of Maintaining Relationship: Moderate

The Compromising style of resolution is characterized by moderately assertive and moderately cooperative behaviors. The person pursues resolution through compromise. This is a concession-oriented style of resolution where each partner concedes to a certain extent. The individual forfeits some of his or her own goals while persuading the other to give up some of their goals. It develops solutions by 'splitting the differences', exchanging concessions, or seeking the middle ground.

Advantages:

When utilizing the compromising style of resolution relationships are maintained for the time being and challenges are temporarily removed. Compromising has the benefit of generating a mutually agreeable solution when there are time constraints. It temporarily relieves the pressure of the challenge.

Disadvantages:

The compromising style of resolution may produce a less

than an ideal outcome in which no one is really satisfied with the result as the outcome does not fully address the complexity of the concerns. Compromise generates a middle-road solution that may be less than fully acceptable to both parties.

Because the solution is less than acceptable or does not fully address the complexity of the concerns it has a tendency to fall apart over the long term.

Long Term Result: Win - Lose, or Lose - Lose

5. COLLABORATION

When Indicated:

Importance of Achieving Your Goal:	High
Importance of Maintaining Relationship:	High

The Collaborating style of resolution is characterized by assertive and cooperative behaviors. The individual expresses his or her concerns and also attempts to understand and recognize the concerns of others.

Collaboration is a discussion-oriented style of resolution where people use listening and communication skills to identify the concerns of both parties so as to generate solutions that meet the needs of both individuals. Collaboration requires the actions of exploring, learning, understanding and deciding.

Advantages:

Collaboration generates win-win solutions where all tensions and negative feelings have been extinguished. It is a process that generates a better understanding between people and creates intimacy.

It creates the most ideal solutions for both parties.

Disadvantages:

The disadvantages of collaboration are that it takes considerable time, effort, skill and commitment. It requires that the person acknowledge challenges in their life. Collaboration requires a high level of skill and a willingness and openness to hear and respect the other's point of view.

This may challenge or threaten one's own understanding of the world, of others, and of oneself.

Long Term Result: Win - Win

Love is an unusual game.
There are either two winners, or none.

Anonymous

PAUSE AND PONDER

☞ **Which style of resolving differences do you use most often?**

☞ **What results do you experience when using this style of resolving differences?**

☞ **Do you use your current style for resolving challenges in all situations? Do you use the same style at work and at home? The same with your boss as with the workers under you? The same with friends as with strangers?**

164

✎ **What styles do you need to add to your personal toolbox?**

SUGGESTIONS FOR CREATING WIN-WIN SOLUTIONS

1. **Encourage the other person to share his or her side of an issue.**

   - Use listening skills to identify and clarify.

   - Check to make sure you have heard and understood correctly.

   - *"Seek first to understand, then to be understood".*

   - *"What I heard you say is…"* and, *"Have I got it right?"*

2. **Ask the other person to listen to your perspective**

    ·   Use 'I' messages.

    ·   Use assertive communication skills.

    ·   Tell your truth as you see it.

    ·   Acknowledge that both perspectives are valid.

3. **Generate a list of possible ideas for a solution.**

    ·   Recognize that both of you have needs/desires which are valid and must be respected.

    ·   Identify solutions that honor both of you.

4. **If a win-win solution is not apparent, identify what else might be required in order to resolve the challenge. You may require more:**

    ·   Information

    ·   Trust

    ·   Energy

    ·   Time

    ·   Skill

    ·   Ideas

Consider taking a break and coming back to the discussion later. This may offer an opportunity to develop new ideas or a different perspective. Consider bringing in other people to aid in the resolution such as friends, ministers, therapists, mediators, or other qualified people and resources.

5. **Agree to disagree at this time and commit to continuing to find a win-win solution.**

Sometimes it's prudent to accept that while there is disagreement at this moment, it isn't necessarily permanent. You can agree to disagree, and express your openness to finding a win-win solution later.

WIN-WIN SOLUTIONS ARE NOT ALWAYS POSSIBLE

The ideal resolution of all kinds of differences is a win-win solution. In this case everybody gains and nobody loses.

Unfortunately this is not always possible. Unequal power relationships (employer-employee; parent-child; offender-victim), time constraints, and other concerns (such as fear) may make win-win solutions unlikely or impossible to attain.

To be effective in dealing with the variety of challenges we encounter in life it is necessary to be aware of and to be skilled in all five styles of resolving differences.

There are times when avoiding is the best style. If my partner is irritable because she is feeling unwell, I might choose to avoid a conflict because it is the best solution at the moment.

Later, when she is feeling better I might choose to work out a better solution that works for both of us.

INTIMACY

When we resolve our differences using collaboration, the outcome is a greater understanding and respect for one another. This increase in understanding and respect contributes to greater intimacy.

Our ultimate goal in creating a better relationship is to increase the amount of intimacy in the relationship.

When we use the word *intimacy* we do not simply mean the degree of sexual contact in a relationship. We use the word intimacy in a much broader context.

Intimacy occurs whenever I allow another to 'see me' for who I am. Intimacy is exactly what the word says: *In-to-me-see.* When we allow another to fully see us for who we are, we are being intimate.

In working with relationships of all kinds, we have seen how people often conceal who they are while in relationship. They conceal what they think and feel for many reasons. One common reason is fear that the other person will not love them if they really knew them. While the act of concealing may sometimes protect us from being hurt, it also insulates us from the experience of being truly loved. This is because when we conceal we make a statement that says *"If you really knew me, you might not love me."*

When we conceal, we hide parts of who we are. The end result is a guarded and cautious relationship where we are constantly vigilant in order to control what the other person knows about us. To have a truly intimate relationship we must tell our truth. We must reveal who we are—what we think, feel and desire in life. When we reveal who we really are and when others continue to love us for who we are, this is when we truly experience love.

Iyania Vanzant, author of *One Day My Soul Just Opened Up*, writes: *"The first way we learn to dishonor ourselves is by not telling the truth. The truth about what we feel, what we want, or what we think."*

Vanzant suggests that we avoid telling the truth because we are afraid of hurting or offending the other person. If this is your reason for concealing your truth, Vanzant has some advice: *"Honor what you feel by saying it the way you would want to hear it. When you say it honestly and with love, your job is over. The only way to learn to trust yourself enough to honor yourself as a divine and unique expression of God is to tell the truth."*

The fact is, being honest might alert us that we need to make significant changes in our life.

It might demand that we confront some painful truths about ourselves or our partner. It might require taking actions and facing all the consequences of those actions. It might mean facing our 'shadow side' that we work to keep hidden from view. When we can't accept these possibilities, we learn to be dishonest, to lie to ourselves, and to conceal the truth. Concealing makes unpleasant things more bearable in the short term.

Unfortunately or fortunately, the truth won't stay hidden. It leaks out in all kind of ways. It leaks out in behaviors such as affairs. It leaks out when we get physically or psychologically ill. It leaks out when people die of a 'broken heart'. It leaks out as anger, resentment, despair and depression.

We believe that some forms of depression are the result of years of depressing one's thoughts and feelings. The pervasiveness of depression in our society may be the result of chronic concealing.

EMOTIONAL BOUNDARIES

One of the reasons many people become hurt in relationships, is because they have poor emotional boundaries. We all know what boundaries are when it comes to property or distinguishing one nation from another. Many of us are unclear what it means to have an *emotional boundary*.

To have an emotional boundary means you have a clear understanding of who is responsible for your emotional well-being and the emotional well-being of others. As we described in Week 2, many people have the belief that when they get into a relationship they are responsible for the happiness of their partner. However, this also means they would be responsible for the sadness experienced by their partner.

If you agree with this belief then you have poor emotional boundaries. You do not know where you stop and the other person begins. You do not know where your responsibility stops and the responsibility of the other person begins.

Having poor emotional boundaries leads to all kinds of difficulty in relationships. This is because whenever you experience pain, sadness or hurt you hold your partner responsible for your feelings. And whenever your partner experiences pain, sadness or hurt they hold you responsible for their feelings.

A person with clear emotional boundaries knows this is not true. A person with clear emotional boundaries cannot be hurt by another. This person knows they are 100% responsible for their feelings.

I can only be insulted with my permission.

This above statement is possible because the individual has a clear understanding of who is responsible for his/her emotional well-being. In the book, *The Four Agreements*, Don Miguel Ruiz states that one of the agreements we ought to make is, "*Do not take anything personally.*"

This is another way of saying we should take responsibility for our emotional well-being rather than allow another to determine our happiness or sadness.

Ray Woollam, author of *On Choosing With A Quiet Mind*, is even more definitive about what it means to have clear emotional boundaries. He suggests your skin is a good way to determine your emotional boundary. If something occurs on the *inside* of your skin, it's your responsibility. If something occurs on the outside of your skin, it's someone else's responsibility.

PAUSE AND PONDER

⤜⤏ **Do you have clear emotional boundaries? Do you know where you start and where you stop?**

⤜⤏ **Whose emotional well-being besides your own do you feel responsible for?**

❧ What is it like to feel responsible for their emotional responses?

❧ Do you truly have the power to make them happy?

SELF RESPONSIBILITY

Each person is responsible for his or her emotional health, as well as their physical, psychological and spiritual health. When you give away responsibility for your health to others, you become sick.

Couples who are healthy (in a relationship sense) are healthy because both people within the relationship are taking care of their own emotional health. They are telling their truth and creating solutions that include *both of their truths.* They are collaborating to create solutions that honor both perspectives.

If you wish to have a better relationship, it is necessary to take responsibility for your own emotional, physical, psychological and spiritual health.

There are many more people trying to meet the right person than trying to become the right person.

Gloria Steinem

RELATIONSHIP STYLES

Each of us has a particular style of being in relationship. These styles are always learned behaviors. See if you can recognize your style from the descriptions below.

The style you have when in a relationship affects your capacity to create intimacy.

The three styles are:

1. **Assertive**

2. **Aggressive**

3. **Passive**

1. ASSERTIVE

In this relationship style opinions, feelings and desires are stated openly and honestly with the intention of revealing who you are, while at the same time respecting the dignity and rights of others.

You make direct statements that clearly state what you mean and what you desire. The use of 'I' messages is common.

The underlying assumption is:

> *"You and I may have our differences, but we are equally entitled to express ourselves to one another."*

The advantages of this style are:

- Active participation in making important decisions
- Getting what you desire
- Maintaining your relationship with others
- The emotional and intellectual satisfaction of respectfully exchanging feelings and ideas
- High esteem
- The potential for a truly intimate relationship

The disadvantages of this style are:

- Requires honesty, personal risk, and courage to reveal yourself to another
- Makes one vulnerable

2. AGGRESSIVE

In this relationship style opinions, feelings and desires are stated honestly but often at the expense of someone else's dignity and rights.

People who engage in this style may use 'loaded' words that can demean or be experienced as 'name calling', accusing or judging. The use of 'You' messages that blame or label is common.

The underlying assumption is:

"I'm superior and/or right and you are inferior and/or wrong."

"I will go to any lengths to get my own way."

The advantages of aggressive behaviors are:

- People often give aggressive individuals what they demand

The disadvantages are:

- Aggressive individuals often alienate people
- People who can't avoid aggressive people may behave dishonestly with them in order to avoid confrontation
- It is impossible to be truly intimate with an aggressive person

3. PASSIVE

In this relationship style opinions, feelings and desires are withheld altogether or expressed indirectly and only in part. There is the use of apologetic words, submissive, veiled meanings, hiding true feelings and rambling. There is often a failure to say what you really mean.

The underlying assumption is:

"I'm not as entitled or as deserving as are you"

or,

"I won't get what I want, so why bother?"

or,

"I don't want to live with the consequences of taking a position."

The advantages of passive communication are:

- It minimizes responsibility for making decisions and the risk of taking a personal stand on an issue.

The disadvantages are:

- A sense of impotence
- Lowered self esteem
- Having to live with the decisions of others
- It is impossible to be truly intimate with a passive person.

PAUSE AND PONDER

☞ **What is your predominant style of relating to others?**

☞ **How has this worked for you?**

☞ **How has it not worked for you?**

☞ **What relationship style would you like to have?**

☞ **What do you need to do to adopt this style of relationship?**

ASSERTIVE = INTIMACY

We hope you noticed that only an assertive person can experience intimacy. The aggressive or passive individual is not able to engage in an intimate relationship with these styles of relating.

On the surface the passive or aggressive relationships may appear to be working, but deep down it's not an honest sharing of one's true self. Rather it's a sharing of the mask we wear.

Many people, however, are not clear on how to be assertive. It is not uncommon for individuals to confuse *assertive* and *aggressive*. Here is a description of assertive behavior, along with some examples.

ASSERTIVENESS

Assertiveness is behavior that enables a person to realize his or her rights by expressing feelings, ideas or thoughts without denying the rights of others.

Assertiveness is:

- the honest expression of one's thoughts, feelings and desires

- letting others know where you stand

- communication utilizing 'I' messages

- a skill which can be learned

- an effective way to reduce anger, resentment and interpersonal anxiety

- behavior that aims at making the power between people equal

- behaviors that open the way for honest and intimate relationships with others

- concerned not only with what you say, but how you say it

- a choice

Assertiveness is not:

- getting your way every time

- a personality trait that some are born with and others are not

- aggressiveness or passive-aggressiveness

- hurtful to others

- appropriate in all situations

The most effective way to communicate assertively is to use 'I' messages. You might recall that we described 'I' messages in Week 3. On the following page is a more detailed description:

'I' MESSAGES

'I' messages are 'the language of responsibility'.

An 'I' message has the following components:

- description of one's feelings and thoughts
- description of the other person's behavior
- the effect the other's behavior has on you
- may include a request of the other person
- does not aim to impose your will or opinion on the other person

Examples of 'I' messages:

"I feel disappointed when you promise to call me and then don't. I feel disrespected and unimportant to you."

"I felt excited when you invited me to the concert with you. I enjoy being with you."

"I feel scared when you drive so fast. I'd like you to slow down when I'm with you."

PAUSE AND PONDER

✎ Create opportunities to practice 'I' messages with three people in your life. Recognize 'I' messages as a means to reveal more of who you are to others.

✎ Notice the impact your 'I' messages are having on those you relate with. Record what you notice.

The following pages have information to support your skill to be an assertive person. These include a listing of Barriers to Assertive Behavior. There is also a listing of *Every Person's Bill of Rights.*

THE KEY IS HOW A MESSAGE IS SENT

Finally, it is important to recognize that you have no control over how your messages will be received by your partner. Your challenge is to let go of trying to control how the message is received and instead, focus on *how the message is sent.*

Work to ensure your messages are sent clearly and are a true expression of your thoughts and feelings *about you.*

It is not nearly so important how a message is received as how it is sent.

Neale Donald Walsch

BARRIERS TO ASSERTIVE BEHAVIOR

Read the list below and identify statements you agree with. Statements with which you agree may indicate your barriers to assertive behavior.

Make an effort to challenge and change these beliefs.

☞ **If I assert myself, others will become angry with me.**

☞ **I'm afraid that if I am open and straightforward with others, I will hurt them.**

✎ If my assertiveness hurts others, I am responsible for their feeling hurt.

✎ It is selfish to turn down legitimate requests by others. If I say 'no', other people will think I don't care about them and they won't like me.

✎ I must avoid making statements and asking questions which might make me look ignorant and stupid, or smart and superior.

✎ Assertive people are cold and uncaring. If I'm assertive, I'll be so unpleasant that people won't like me.

✎ It's better to have people like you, even if they don't really know who you are.

✎ If I'm going to be assertive, I always have to know what I want; I must always know the right answer.

✎ Assertive and aggressive behaviors are the same thing; I don't want to be aggressive.

EVERY PERSON'S BILL OF RIGHTS

Here is a commonly shared declaration of rights for you to use as inspiration in writing your own Bill of Rights:

1. The right to be treated with respect.

2. The right to have and express your own feelings and ideas.

3. The right to be listened to and taken seriously.

4. The right to decide what is right for yourself.

5. The right to say 'no' without feeling guilty.

6. The right to ask for what you want (realizing that the other has the right to refuse).

7. The right to get what you pay for.

8. The right to fail.

9. The right to ask for information from others.

10. The right to choose not to be assertive.

Read the list daily. Post the Bill of Rights on your bathroom mirror or other visible location to remind you of some of your rights as a human being, including your rights as an equal partner in a relationship.

SUMMARY

During Week 4 you have learned much about your particular style of being in a relationship. You have learned whether you tend to be predominantly passive, aggressive or assertive when relating with others.

You have learned your preferred style of resolving differences in your relationships.

We trust that you have also learned some of what it takes to create more intimacy in your relationships. We hope you are telling your truth using 'I' messages, and creating solutions that honor your truth.

You have also developed an appreciation for the value of differences, and discovered how we create our experience of an event depending on the meaning we assign to it.

In Week 5 we will provide exercises for you and your partner to do together. These exercises provide additional information about how you behave in relationships.

But for the remainder of this week, continue to practice the behaviors of *truth telling*, *assertiveness* and *collaboration*.

PAUSE AND PONDER

↩ **What ideas stood out the most for you this week?**

↩ **What ideas were new for you?**

↩ **What ideas were challenging and difficult for you to accept or understand?**

↩ **What did you learn about yourself?**

≼⇔ **What did you learn about your partner?**

CONGRATULATIONS!

You have completed **Week 4** in your journey to a Better Relationship.

⌇WEEK 5:

*Just because someone doesn't love you
the way you want them to,
doesn't mean they don't love you
with all they have.*

Anonymous

WELCOME TO WEEK FIVE.

Be encouraged: we're already at the halfway mark! Well done for sticking with it so far.

Last week we discussed the idea that relationships are a blessing because they provide an opportunity to know who you are. We explained that relationships provide opportunities to experience ourselves as kind, loving, generous, patient and understanding, or as impatient, jealous, fearful and insensitive. We pointed out that you can't know yourself fully while living in isolation.

Finally, we explored the ideas people have about differences; we encouraged you to identify your preferred style for resolving differences; and we helped you identify your primary way of relating to others.

This week you will be provided with a number of exercises to help you and your partner get to know each other better. This knowledge will help you create greater intimacy (in-to-me-see). Each of these exercises is an opportunity to understand your partner and yourself more fully.

Everyone sees, experiences and understands the world in uniquely different ways. Each of us has our own particular way of living and loving. We don't all speak the same language when it comes to love. And so, if we are to get along, we had better understand, appreciate and behave in ways that effectively communicate our love to one another.

THE FIVE LANGUAGES OF LOVE

One of our favorite exercises is *The Five Languages of Love*, based on the work of Gary Chapman. In his book, Chapman presents the idea that individuals experience love in different ways. He identifies the following five different ways of experiencing and expressing love:

- Words of Affirmation

- Quality Time

- Giving and Receiving Gifts

- Acts of Service

- Physical Touch

To learn more about Chapman's work and to assess your love language and that of your partner, we encourage you to complete the free assessment available on *The Five Languages of Love* website: http://www.5lovelanguages.com/assessments/love

It takes only 10-15 minutes, but to whet your appetite, we have tried to interpret some key points from his work into just a few sentences below:

Words of Affirmation

If this is your love language, you love compliments. Hearing the words, *"I love you"* or *"You look beautiful"* mean a lot. The use of words in expressing love touch you the most deeply of all the five languages.

Quality Time

If Quality Time is your love language, you enjoy your partner's undivided attention. You feel special when your partner clears a space in his or her day and uses it to just be with you. What you do is not as important as being able to do it together.

Receiving Gifts

This person feels special when their partner puts thought and effort into buying just the right gift that shows they know and appreciate you. You can hardly wait for birthdays and anniversaries as a way to express your love to your partner with just the perfect gift.

Acts of Service

For this person, something as simple as vacuuming the floors can be an expression of love. They love to hear, "*Let me do that for you.*" This person is especially moved if their partner does something for them that they know is not their joy but they do it anyway as an expression of their love and appreciation.

Physical Touch

This language isn't just about the bedroom. A person whose primary language is Physical Touch loves hugs, pats on the back, holding hands, and thoughtful touches on the arm, shoulder, or face. Just cuddling up on the couch warms their heart.

As mentioned above, we encourage you to learn more about the Five Languages of Love, including completing the free online assessment. It will help identify your primary love language, what it means, and how you can use it to connect with your loved one with intimacy and fulfillment.

TRYING TO COMMUNICATE IN THE WRONG LANGUAGE

When a couple experience problems in their relationship, one explanation may be that one or both are communicating love in the 'wrong' language. By the wrong language we mean a language that doesn't work for their partner.

Most people make the error of expressing love in the language they prefer, rather than the language their partner prefers.

The impact of this is evident if you think about travelling in a foreign country and attempting to communicate with someone in your language rather than the language of the person you are speaking with. The end result is lots of shrugs and smiles but no real communication.

Couples who don't recognize that love has many languages struggle in their ability to communicate love to their partner. It isn't that they don't love their partner; rather, the message of love simply isn't getting through. They are communicating love in a language that is not well understood by their partner.

BARB AND DOUGLAS

An example of this concept was demonstrated during a recent counseling session Ted had with a couple we'll call Barb and Douglas. During the session Barb lamented to Douglas, *"You never tell me you love me!"*

Douglas, appearing genuinely confused, replied: *"What do you mean, I don't tell you I love you? Each week I bring my paycheck home and put it on the dining room table. What do you think that means?"*

From this brief information it is apparent that Barb's preferred love language is different from Douglas's.

Barb's preferred language seems to be 'words of affirmation'. She longs to hear the words *"I love you."*

Douglas's preferred language appears to be 'acts of service'. Going to work each day and bringing home a paycheck is Douglas's way of saying *"I love you."*

Douglas's love, as expressed by his earnings, has not been received by Barb. As a result, Barb fails to benefit from Douglas's messages of love.

One of the reasons for Barb and Douglas's confusion is because this notion of love having many languages is not common knowledge.

When we speak English to a non-English speaking person we know immediately whether we are being understood. This is because we look for and receive feedback that tells us whether our message is being received.

In relationships, however, it is not always obvious that a message of love is not being received.

This is because most people assume there is only one language of love. It doesn't occur to them that love has different 'languages'.

While Barb and Douglas truly love one another, their messages of love are not being communicated effectively. And if nothing changes to improve this couple's effectiveness in communicating their love for one another, this relationship could dissolve. Each will complain of not being loved by the other.

At the same time both individuals will feel hurt that their partner is not responding to their expressions of love.

It's important to be aware of both our own preferred language of love, and the language preferred by our partner. The reason is so we can *invite* love in the love language we experience most deeply, and also *communicate* our love to our partner in the language our partner best understands.

A message of love sent in the wrong language has the effect of not being sent at all.

Note: No love language is better or 'more correct' than another. Each is perfectly valid; it's an individual style. Honor and celebrate your differences. Respect each other's way of experiencing love.

Take time now to clarify what your preferred love language looks and sounds like.

Invite your partner to also share what his or her preferred love language looks and sounds like.

Use this opportunity to discover what makes each of your hearts sing!

Enjoy doing this exercise!

You might even consider making this the focus of a date with your partner.

PAUSE AND PONDER

☞ **My preferred love language is:**

☞ **How this expression of love looks (or sounds) is:**

☞ **My partner's preferred love language is:**

✎ **How this expression of love looks (or sounds) is:**

PERSONALITY TYPING

Most people readily accept that men and women experience the world differently. John Gray's book *Men Are From Mars, Women are From Venus* has been useful in articulating gender differences. In truth there are more than two ways (male and female) of seeing the world.

Another well-known way to help people better understand one another is 'True Colors', a tool designed to identify one's predominant personality type. According to this model, there are four different personality types, to which the creators have assigned the colors blue, orange, green and gold.

If you are interested in learning more about the True Colors model, we encourage you to check your local city or community for professionals offering workshops, or to visit their website[4].

---

4   http://www.true-colors.com

WE ARE ALL DIFFERENT

The goal of these exercises (and others like them) is to more fully appreciate how <u>each one of us perceives and experiences the world in slightly different ways</u>. We also communicate our feelings differently, and resonate better with certain methods of emotional communication.

John Gray sees men and women as coming from different planets; *True Colors* suggests there are four different ways of engaging the world. Other personality-typing methods such as the Myers Briggs Personality Inventory identify even more.

Which methods you choose to use is not that important. What is important is to understand that the differences these tools identify may account for some of the challenges you experience in your relationship.

By understanding who you are and what makes your heart sing, and understanding who your partner is and what makes his or her heart sing, you increase your ability to live together in a joyful, harmonious and respectful way.

DO THIS FUN EXERCISE

On the following pages is an exercise to help you identify your personality type. Use this exercise to get to know yourself and your partner better.

Share your results with your partner. Invite your partner to share his or her results with you.

There is no right or wrong personality type. There are many personality types, and all of them are equally valid.

A word of caution about personality typing exercises: they are simply ways to help clarify your personality type. Do not allow the questionnaire to decide who you are. Rather use it as a tool to become curious about who you are and who your partner is. These kinds of tools are only valuable to the degree they are useful to you.

Once you have read the description of your personality type and that of your partner, see if this explains some of the experiences you've had in your relationship. Notice if the description feels right to you. If it doesn't fit, read the remaining descriptions and identify the description which best describes you. This is likely to be your personality type.

WHO ARE YOU?

Directions: Read the words below. Identify the cluster of three words (i.e. the vertical column in each grouping) that *best* describes you. <u>Score this cluster as a '4'</u>. Then identify the cluster of words that is *least* like you. Score this cluster as a '1'.

Review the remaining cluster of words and assign a 3 to the cluster that is next most like you. Score the remaining cluster of words as a 2. Ensure that you have assigned a number to all four clusters of words. Then move on to the next grouping of words. When you have finished assigning a number to all the clusters, total up the vertical columns.

Scoring Key:

"Most like me" = 4   "Least like me" = 1

Example:

Funny	Sensitive	Serious	Playful
Laughs	Tender	Worries	Fun loving
Superficial	Emotional	Thinker	Active
④	②	③	①

In this example, I felt the vertical cluster that least described me was the last one: *Playful*, *Fun-loving*, and *Active*. I marked that as a '1'. The one most like me was the first cluster: *Funny, Laughs, Superficial*; I marked that a '4'. Get it?

Good. Now try these for yourself:

Real	Loyal	Flexible	Active
Agreeable	Traditional	Resourceful	Daring
Caring	Responsible	Capable	Spontaneous
◯	◯	◯	◯

Unique	Practical	Curious	Competitive
Affectionate	Sensible	Conceptual	Impatient
Open	Dependable	Knowledgeable	Impactful
◯	◯	◯	◯

Devoted	Parental	Theoretical	Realistic
Sensitive	Reasonable	Questioning	Open-Minded
Poetic	Organized	Creative	Adventurous
◯	◯	◯	◯
Tender	Concerned	Determined	Opportunistic
Many Ideas	Methodical	Complex	Impulsive
Dramatic	Cooperative	Calm	Fun
◯	◯	◯	◯
Energetic	Orderly	Thinking	Exciting
Warm	Conventional	Principled	Courageous
Sympathetic	Caring	Rational	Skillful
◯	◯	◯	◯

TOTALS

TYPE A	TYPE B	TYPE C	TYPE D
☐	☐	☐	☐

Scoring: The box with the highest score indicates your personality type. If you have two scores which are equal or very close, read the descriptions for both types and identify the type that describes you the best.

TYPE A: HEART BASED/FEELING

Basic Philosophy: To love and be loved

- naturally loving, nurturing, supportive
- good people skills
- sensitive, intuitive, empathic
- soft and gentle demeanor
- calming effect
- loves unconditionally
- least judgmental of all personality types
- affirming
- communicates from the heart
- talks about their feelings
- takes things personally
- doesn't take criticism well
- wears their hearts on their sleeves
- likes helping others

Well-Known Type A personalities

- Oprah
- Carl Rogers
- Mother Teresa
- Princess Diana

- Meg Ryan
- Mahatma Ghandi

TYPE B: ORGANIZED/ORDERLY

Basic Philosophy: Planner

- quiet, conservative type
- neat, clean, well groomed, dressed appropriately
- doesn't need to stand out or be noticed
- dependable, reliable, will do what they say they will do
- on time; likes punctuality
- sets clock ten minutes ahead to arrive early
- hates being late—will not go if late
- organized; keeps things neat and tidy
- their home looks like no one lives there
- everything is in its right place
- cleanliness is next to godliness
- finds it difficult to sit and relax if dishes undone or dirty house
- insists on proper behavior
- does things the right way

- strong opinions about what is right and wrong

- books, CD's, clothes in order

- likes predictability

- doesn't like surprises or spontaneity

- will park car in the same spot if possible

- will sit in the same seat in class

- serious

- perfectionist, detailed

- worries a lot

- cautious, methodological

- is not a risk taker

- needs information in an orderly and sequential way

- needs all the facts to make a decision

- likes calendars, date books, lists

- strong work ethic

Well Known Type B personalities

- Queen Elizabeth
- Winston Churchill
- Henry Ford
- George Washington
- Florence Nightingale

TYPE C: HEAD BASED/THINKING

Basic Philosophy: Knowledge is power

- deep and brilliant thinkers
- intelligent, clever, wise, witty
- achieved good grades in school
- natural leaders
- bored by mundane conversations or idle chit chat
- prefers stimulating conversations
- enjoys mental challenges—puzzle, chess, problems
- perfectionists—need to be good at what they do
- wants to do it right or not at all
- has high standards
- tends to be scientists, university professors, researchers
- likes to ask questions
- is bored with repetition—wants to move on
- does not tolerate uninformed, ignorant people
- become restless quickly
- likes arguments—good debater, negotiator
- likes to analyze things

- takes things apart and puts them back together
- curious
- needs time to think before they respond
- self assured, confident
- not easily influenced by the opinions of others
- tells the truth (so be careful asking for their opinion)
- will defend their ideas
- doesn't show emotions easily
- cool, calm, collected composure—passive expressions
- difficult to read emotions

Well Known Type C personalities

- Steve Jobs
- Benjamin Franklin
- Einstein
- Mr. Spock (Star Trek)
- Hillary Clinton
- Margaret Thatcher
- Socrates
- Thomas Edison

TYPE D: SPONTANEOUS/PLAYFUL

Basic Philosophy: Where's the action?

- upbeat, light hearted, fun loving
- laughing, having a good time
- centre of attention
- extroverted
- likes to entertain
- lives for today
- doesn't save, store, or prepare
- lives life in the present
- doesn't take life seriously
- child-like
- spontaneous, action oriented
- Peter Pans
- never wants to grow up or grow old
- free spirits
- flamboyant
- high energy level
- does several things at one time
- impulsive
- blunt, not brutal
- extravagant gifts, big parties

- moves quickly, don't stay in one place long
- restless and bored easily
- likes change, excitement, unpredictability

Well Known Type D personalities

- John F. Kennedy
- Donald Trump
- Bill Clinton
- Bart Simpson
- Amelia Earhart
- Elvis Presley
- Madonna

PAUSE AND PONDER

✑ **What appears to be your personality type?**

✑ **Briefly describe your personality.**

✑➤ What is your partner's personality type?

✑➤ Briefly describe your partner's personality.

✑➤ Identify an aspect of your relationship that could be described as challenging. Does personality typing help to explain why this is a challenge?

How might your understanding of personality typing change the way you relate with your partner now?

Personality typing provides information that helps explain the differences that exist between people. It offers clues and insights into our own and another's behavior. It helps us to better understand why we behave as we do.

Having different personality types does not necessarily mean a couple is not compatible.

It does mean, however, that they see and experience the world in different ways and will need to be sensitive to their partner's perspective.

PERSONALITIES UNDER STRESS

Personality typing also predicts how different personality types react under stress. While these are generalizations, this information may be useful in understanding how you and your partner respond to challenges in life.

Personality Type	Response under Stress
Type A	Goes along
Type B	Becomes Autocratic
Type C	Avoids
Type D	Attacks

Does this information help to explain your behavior and that of your partner? Each of these tools is best embraced with an attitude of openness, curiosity, and a desire to know yourself and your partner better. Our purpose in encouraging you to play with these methods is to help you and your partner become more intimate—to see 'into' one's self and into others, and to allow others to see into you.

Getting to know yourself and your life partner is an exciting time. It is what makes the courting stage of a relationship interesting. You can re-create that initial excitement and enthusiasm again. Invite yourself and your partner to dream, create and to design your life again and again. When you open up your passion for life, love flows.

GETTING TO KNOW YOURSELF AND YOUR PARTNER

There are many other ways of getting to know yourself and your partner better. What would like to know about your partner?

What it is your partner would like to know about you?

What questions do you both have?

Write your questions down. Then arrange a time with your partner to ask your questions.

We have provided a few examples to help you to get you started and help develop your own questions:

↝ **What do you want to experience in your life now?**

✎ **What would you like to accomplish in the next ten years?**

✎ **What brings you joy? Excitement?**

⊰⊱ **What makes your heart sing?**

⊰⊱ **If you could do whatever you wanted, what would you do?**

➤ **Where would you like to live? Why?**

➤ **If you lived somewhere else, how would your life be different than what it is now?**

✍ **What dreams do you have?**

✍ **What regrets do you have? What do you wish you had done differently?**

✍ **If you had all the money you desired, what would you buy?**

✍ **If you had all the time you desired, what would you do?**

✍ **If you could give yourself a present, what would it be?**

SUMMARY

We hope that this has been an interesting and exciting week for you and your partner. By exploring your personality types and finding out how each of you prefers to communicate in a loving relationship, and by asking and answering some fairly intimate questions about your dreams for now the future, you and your partner have shared some intimate moments.

Notice what intimacy feels like. Notice that it starts with you allowing others to 'in-to-me-see'. Does this excite you? Does it feel a little scary? Does it motivate you to reveal more than you have in the past?

It is our hope that this week has opened up new possibilities for you and your partner and stimulated excitement and passion in your relationship and in your life.

In Week 6, we will ask you to share your thoughts of your ideal relationship with your partner. Then we'll help you identify a direction for your future and develop a plan of action.

PAUSE AND PONDER

✍ **What ideas stood out the most for you this week?**

✍ **What ideas were new for you?**

☞ **What ideas were challenging and difficult for you to accept or understand?**

☞ **What did you learn about yourself?**

☞ **What did you learn about your partner?**

CONGRATULATIONS!

You have completed **Week 5** in your journey to a Better Relationship.

≋WEEK 6:

The secret of getting ahead
is getting started.
The secret of getting started is breaking
your complex overwhelming tasks
into small manageable tasks
and then starting on the first one.

Mark Twain

WELCOME TO WEEK SIX.

Last week you got to know your partner better. We trust that you now have a greater appreciation of how unique and special each of you is. We also trust that you and your partner have had more practice in listening and sharing information.

This week, we invite you to share your vision of your ideal relationship with each other.

So far, most of the work we have asked you to do was internal—inside your head and heart. You learned about the attributes required for an intimate relationship; identified what your ideal relationship looks and feels like; were given information about listening skills and communicating effectively; and you were provided with information on how to resolve differences when they arise in your relationship.

Now is the opportunity to put your knowledge and skills into action. Knowledge is important. But *it is only by taking action that your relationship will improve.*

INTIMACY (IN-TO-ME-SEE)

This week we invite you to get together with your partner and share your honest thoughts and feelings. Share what you like and what your ideal relationship looks like. It may have been a long time since you and your partner had this level of sharing…. or perhaps you have never had anything even close to it.

You might have shared this kind of information at the beginning of your relationship. To some degree, we all do this with prospective partners to determine our level of compatibility. When we first meet a potential partner it is common to talk a lot about our goals and dreams for the future, our career, passions, interests, needs and desires.

Unfortunately, many couples stop having these kinds of conversations once they become committed to one another. One explanation is that couples assume they now know everything there is to know about one another. Another explanation is that couples stop talking out of fear they might discover something that threatens their compatibility.

Consciously and unconsciously, some individuals worry and ask themselves questions like:

"What will happen if our interests are no longer the same?"

"What will happen if our directions change?"

"What if we want different dreams?"

"What will this mean for the future of our relationship?"

Many people, once they have committed themselves to another, hold this commitment as more valuable than their own happiness, joy or goals in life. Then, out of fear that they might hear something that could challenge their commitment to the relationship, they cover their eyes and ears.

When a couple stops sharing with each other, the intimacy diminishes.

AFFAIRS

As mentioned before, intimacy is not the same as sexuality, although lovemaking is a natural extension of being intimate. When the 'in-to-me-see' stops, the lovemaking tends to stop as well. We regularly listen to couples who share more about what they want in the decoration of their home or what furniture or car to buy, than about who they are deep down inside as individuals.

The result is their love affair with each other becomes transferred elsewhere—their house, car, career, children, sports or hobbies.

In our experience, 'affairs' seldom begin with sexual relations with someone else. Rather, a sexual affair often comes near the end of the affair. Affairs usually begin with one's home, career, hobby or children. If this seems a strange notion, consider for a moment what an affair is. An affair is anything that draws the energy and attention away from the primary relationship. Typically we see this as being another sexual partner. But we invite you to consider an understanding of affairs beyond this narrow perspective.

Notice how many couples you know have stopped investing time and energy in their relationship. It's almost as if the couple decides, "Well, *now that we've got that taken care of, it's time to focus on other things.*" The energy that went into creating the relationship is directed elsewhere. In our view it's possible to have an affair with television, the computer, playing or watching sports, one's children, and anything that becomes the primary focus of one's energy, attention and passion.

We have met many couples where, for example, the husband was having an affair with his work while his wife was having an affair with their children. The only relationship the couple maintained was a business relationship, a kind of mutual arrangement where the business of buying a home, paying the mortgage, buying groceries and clothing, bringing up the children and the completion of everyday tasks occurred.

AVOIDING INTIMACY

Harville Hendrix, in his classic book, *Getting the Love You Want,* identifies a common behavior that occurs when couples are struggling in their relationship. His observation is that many couples have what he calls an 'invisible divorce'. They structure their lives in such a way as to avoid each other and begin to seek pleasure and satisfaction outside of their relationship.

Hendrix is not talking about affairs as we commonly understand them, but rather is recognizing that many couples use common, every day activities as a way to escape the relationship. He routinely asks his clients a simple question: *"What does your spouse do to avoid you?"*

The answers are all too familiar. Hendrix has generated a list of over three hundred different answers. See if you recognize yourself in some of these behaviors:

- Reading romance novels
- Watching TV
- Running
- Exercising
- Talking on the phone
- Playing video games
- Surfing the internet
- Using social media
- Working in the garage, basement, back yard

- Sleeping
- Going fishing
- Going shopping
- Smoking
- Drinking
- Doing crossword puzzles

Are there ways that you consistently and routinely avoid your partner? Do you seek your satisfaction and pleasure outside of the relationship? If so, it is only a matter of time before the relationship suffers as a result of the lack of time and attention. Just as a seed needs watering in order to grow, so too our relationships need watering. They need time and loving attention if we expect them to grow.

PAUSE AND PONDER

✍ **What do you do to avoid your partner?**

LACK OF INTIMACY

We believe the root cause of an affair is a lack of *in-to-me-see* in the relationship. These people have stopped revealing who they are to each other. They no longer allow their partner to see 'into' them. At some point they stop sharing who they are and how they are growing and evolving.

This lack of in-to-me-see can occur when individuals become afraid of what might happen if their partner saw into them, saw their thoughts and feelings, heard their change in goals, heard their discontent, and heard the change in passions or dreams.

Fear, and the concealing that results from fear, causes relationships to become distant, and to become a business relationship or a 'relationship of convenience' rather than an intimate relationship.

IT TAKES COURAGE

During this week we invite you to risk becoming intimate again with your partner. We recognize this takes courage. It may be that it's been a long time since you last shared your innermost thoughts and feelings with your partner. It may be that it's been a long time since your partner shared his or her innermost thoughts and feelings with you.

You might anticipate that your partner will not be pleased with your current thoughts and feelings. It's possible that you might not be pleased with what your partner has to share with you. And, it's possible that you and your partner are simply out of practice.

Now is a decision point in your relationship.

This is the time to consciously choose to reveal who you are, or to conceal who you are; to be honest with your partner, or to be dishonest.

Ultimately a relationship cannot sustain itself if honesty is not present. When you share your life with your partner in a spirit of honesty, and when you do so with respect and acceptance of who he or she is now, your relationship will grow in intimacy even if you and your partner discover you are on different paths in life.

The choice is simple. If you carry on concealing, you deny both yourself and your partner the opportunity to have an intimate relationship: a relationship where both of you grow to your highest potential; where each of you can be more together than you are apart.

THIS WEEK'S GOALS

Our goals this week are to have you:

- Meet with your partner and share your ideal relationship
- Assess the degree of shared vision
- Identify your future direction
- Commit your intentions to paper

These goals may seem a little overwhelming, yet they are all manageable. Lee shares some advice from his book *How to Escape your Comfort Zones*:

It's not so difficult to eat an elephant…
just take it one forkful at a time.

The first step is to break down what may seem complex and overwhelming into smaller, more manageable steps, then to start with the first step.

We see the steps as follows:

Step 1: **Set a time for sharing**

Step 2: **Prepare yourself for the sharing**

Step 3: **The sharing**

Step 4: **Reflect on the sharing**

Step 5:	Assess the degree of shared vision
Step 6:	Identify your direction
Step 7:	Declare yourself to your partner

STEP 1: SET A TIME FOR SHARING

Your first task is to set a time to share with your partner. Even though your partner is reading this same material and has been instructed to set a time with you, don't sit back and wait. This is an opportunity to take 100% responsibility for creating the relationship you want.

We suggest you identify a time of day and a day of the week when you and your partner will have time alone together. This may require some planning and coordination of your schedules. It may be necessary to hire a sitter for your children. It may be necessary to take an afternoon off work.

You may decide to arrange for a special setting to have this conversation—a quiet restaurant, a retreat setting, or a walk on the beach so the two of you can concentrate one hundred percent of your attention on one another.

What is essential is that you and your partner have an opportunity for intimate, uninterrupted conversation. We suggest you intentionally invite your partner to an opportunity to share your thoughts and feelings about your ideal relationship. Below is one suggestion of how you might arrange this meeting.

234

SUGGESTION FOR INVITATION

You might consider writing your partner a letter, something like the one provided below. Write it on fancy paper, put the letter in a nice envelope, and place it on your partner's pillow together with a flower, a chocolate, or a small gift.

You might want to take into consideration their preferred language of love.

> *Dear .... (Your partner's name, or Hi Sweetie, or whatever your term of endearment may be),*
>
> *As you know, I have been reading the book <u>8 Weeks to a Better Relationship</u>. It has helped me to acknowledge my thoughts and feelings about me, you, and us. Now the time has come to share my thoughts and feelings with you, and hearing from you about yours.*
>
> *My intention in getting together and sharing this information with you is so that we can identify what we can do to make our relationship better.*
>
> *I really look forward to this as a positive step forward in our relationship.*
>
> *I think a good time to meet would be ------------------*
>
> *My suggestion for a good place to meet is ----------------*
>
> *Does this arrangement work for you?*

Thank you for agreeing to meet with me to hear my thoughts and feelings. I look forward to sharing with you.

Love,

--------------------- (sign your name)

Date

If you prefer, use your imagination to make up your own invitation.

Your invitation might be spoken rather than written.

Be sure to communicate your intent to make your relationship better. This is an opportunity for you to share with your partner— to have an experience of 'in-to-me-see'.

STEP TWO: PREPARE YOURSELF FOR THE SHARING

Once you have established a time and place the next step is to prepare yourself for this sharing. Do you feel nervous, excited, scared?

Good!

This is an indication you are doing something different. This is an indication that you intend to be intimate.

Whenever we start down a new path, it always feels strange and unfamiliar. We often experience a sense of anxiety or confusion.

If you experience this, don't let these feelings deter you. These feelings are a sure sign that you are breaking out of your old comfort zone and about to do something different. Remember the quotation from Week 1 :

If I want something I've never had before,
I must be willing to do something I've never done before.

A question to ask yourself is this: "*Am I willing to do what it takes to get what I want?*"

Is this beginning to feel similar to your first dates with your partner? In many ways it *is* like having a first date all over again. Notice your feelings of nervousness or excitement.

Don't judge your feelings or allow yourself to go into fear. Simply feel your feelings. Enjoy them. Notice that you feel alive!

You may want to take time to journal or write a poem about what you are feeling at this time. You might even decide to write your thoughts and feelings down in the form of a letter to your partner and let him or her read it when you get together.

Review the work you did in Week 1. You may want to re-read the chapter. When you have a clear sense of your worthiness, choice, and responsibility, you are able to be confident in your ability to create a better relationship.

Know that you deserve to have the best life has to offer. Know that you have choice. Take 100% responsibility for your happiness

Next, review the notes you made in Week 2 where you listed the qualities of your ideal relationship. See if there are any changes or additions you want to make now. Feel free to add or change anything you have written previously.

Remember, this is a living document, an ongoing process of discovery. It is a process of becoming clearer about who you are and what you desire in life. You may notice that you are very clear and certain about what you want. You might also notice that your ideas keep changing.

You may want to prepare written notes for your sharing with your partner. For some people it is more effective to write a letter and to give it to their partner (or read it out loud to them).

Verbal communication requires a high level of skill, and it is not uncommon when communicating verbally, to get distracted by something the other person says or does. Some people get so distracted that they forget what they wanted to say. And sometimes one's thoughts simply don't come out right when expressed verbally.

If you think you will find it difficult to communicate verbally with your partner, take time to draft a letter. Then when you meet, share your letter with your partner. After your partner has read it, the two of you can discuss what you have written.

This meeting is an opportunity for you to test your listening and communication skills. Remember, listening is primarily about *understanding*. Seek first to understand, then to be understood.

When it is time for you to share information, ensure that your messages are expressed as 'I' messages. Allow your partner to reveal what they think and feel through their own 'I' messages.

Take responsibility for revealing who you are. Make it safe for your partner to reveal who he/she is.

Trust in your ability to resolve differences satisfactorily. Come from a place of trust and confidence in your future. Know that you have the capability to make your life work for you, to be happy, peaceful and joyful regardless of what your partner decides.

Remember that only you are responsible for your happiness. You are not responsible for your partner's happiness. Nor does your happiness come from your partner.

If you have been living with fear, now is the time to decide to stop fearing. Fear paralyses and gets in your way. When you build confidence and trust in yourself, your fear subsides.

OK, this is the big moment.

You're fully prepared. You've reviewed your notes. It's time to meet with your partner and do some beautiful sharing!

STEP 3: THE SHARING

The goal of this step is to share intimate aspects of yourself with your partner. The sharing of your goals and dreams is an act of intimacy. Remember, the purpose of this sharing is to *reveal your ideas about your future*, not to resolve the past. It is a visioning process, not a finger-pointing process.

The sharing is an opportunity to inform each other about who each of you is now. Any discussion should be to clarify what has been stated, not to defend one's ideas. If you notice yourself disagreeing or arguing, recognize that the two of you have gotten off track. This is supposed to be a time of sharing dreams and goals and of getting to know each other better.

We encourage you to use the communication skills described in Week 3. Specifically we suggest you use the phrase, *"What I heard you say is ......"* and, *"Have I got it right?"* to acknowledge what you think you heard your partner saying.

Use this process until your partner has confirmed that you have understood their message accurately and they have nothing else they wish to share with you.

Once you have reached this level of shared understanding, the purpose of your meeting has been achieved.

Thank your partner for opening themselves to you. Give yourself credit for this important step that you have taken toward a more intimate relationship.

STEP FOUR: REFLECT ON THE SHARING

Now comes the work of considering what you have heard and learned about your partner. We suggest you and your partner take some time to reflect upon what has been shared. Allow the information to settle for a few days. The sharing you and your partner have done is an act of intimacy and improves your understanding and connection with one another.

Notice your thoughts and feelings. What emotions have been stirred up? Excitement? Hope? Love? Fear? Anxiety? Confusion? Disappointment?

Do your best to identify what you are feeling. Be aware that you may be feeling many different, even conflicting feelings at the same time. The better you are able to identify your feelings, the more manageable they become.

☞ **I'm feeling:**

☞ **I feel this way because:**

STEP 5: ASSESS THE DEGREE OF SHARED VISION

What is the degree of overlap in your visions? Is there a high degree of overlap or a low degree of overlap?

Is there enough overlap for this relationship to be viable or does it seem as though the two of you are headed in different directions?

Resist the temptation to minimize your own desires and goals to match those of your partner.

Review the information on shared visions earlier in the book. How do your partner's wishes fit with your list of preferences and non-negotiables identified in Week 2? Look within.

What does your intuition tell you?

What is the feeling in your gut?

Is there excitement? Hope? Confidence?

Or is there doubt? Disappointment?

Concern? Sadness?

Your feelings are a good indicator of the truth. To quantify those feelings, try to assign a percentage of overlap between your own vision and that of your partner:

My assessment of our current degree of overlap in terms of our shared vision is:

------------%.

(The higher the percentage, the greater the overlap)

 242

On a sliding scale it would look like this:

RELATIONSHIP BAROMETER

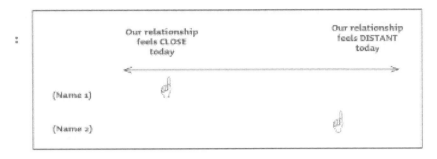

Using a pencil, draw a large dot on the point of the scale which best represents your current position. You could also use a small sticker.

Considering the above assessment, in my opinion there is (check one):

( )   More than enough overlap to have a viable relationship

( )   Sufficient overlap to have a viable relationship

( )   Insufficient overlap to have a viable relationship

( )   Definitely not enough overlap to have a viable relationship

STEP 6: IDENTIFY YOUR DIRECTION

Your next task is to identify your direction. Ultimately, there are only three possible options. They are:

1. **Do more of the same**
2. **Improve your relationship**
3. **End your relationship**

The direction you decide will be determined by two considerations:

1. **The degree of shared vision for your future**
2. **Your confidence in achieving this vision with your partner**

Only you can decide whether the level of shared vision and confidence is high enough for you to invest further time and energy in the relationship. Similarly, only your partner can decide for himself or herself whether the level of shared vision and confidence is high enough for them to invest further in the relationship.

For some people it is enough to have shared understanding in certain core areas such as children, parenting, fidelity, and financial responsibility. This core sharing might make a lack of overlap in other areas acceptable.

The differences may represent some of your growing areas.

For other people, a higher level of shared understanding and commitment is necessary to sustain the relationship.

If your relationship is to be viable, *both* partners must be satisfied with the vision for the relationship. A relationship cannot sustain itself when only one of you is content with the vision and direction.

<u>Both partners</u> need to be satisfied with the degree of overlap, and also with the compromises where there is little or no overlap.

Just like the three-legged race we talked about in Week 2, both partners must be headed in the same direction. If there is a significant difference in direction, couples typically engage in a tug of war, attempting to tug the other over to their side. This strategy will not create a harmonious relationship. Instead, it creates a relationship that is constantly under tension and where each is being pulled in a direction they don't wish to go.

STEP SEVEN: DECLARE YOURSELF TO YOUR PARTNER

Your final task this week is to commit your intentions to paper. *Once you have identified the direction you intend to pursue, you need to declare your intentions.*

Just as you publicly declared your intentions to marry (if you are married) as a way of giving your commitment more power, so too declaring your intentions at this stage gives them more power. But no matter what you have decided, *it is important to commit your intentions to paper.*

Expressing your commitment in writing and signing your name is the first step in taking action and moving forward. Research on change indicates the more clearly you make a commitment, the more powerful your actions become. If you keep your decision to yourself, it loses its power. You also fail to access the support of those around you to help you with your decision. By writing your decision down and signing your name, you indicate to yourself and to your partner the seriousness of your decision. The message you're sending is, *"I'm committed to moving in this direction."*

On the following pages we have provided three possible declarations you can make to your partner. Read each declaration carefully and decide the direction that feels best for you at this time. Then arrange a time to share your declaration with your partner in a manner suitable for the decision you have made.

You may want to do it alone, on a hilltop, a quiet table at a romantic restaurant, in the privacy of your own home, together with a trusted friend, at a therapist's office, or whatever works for you. If you decide not to make a decision at this time, you are still choosing. Recognize that *you are choosing to do more of the same.*

POSSIBILITY 1: DO MORE OF THE SAME

If your decision is to do 'more of the same', we suggest you write out a declaration similar to the one below. The significance of this step is to firmly and consciously acknowledge the direction you are headed.

Use this as a template to create your own declaration.

It is important to carefully read and think about each of the options below, and consider all the implications of your decision.

Dear .... (Your partner's name, or Hi Sweetie, or whatever your own term of endearment may be),

As you know, I have been reading the book 8 Weeks to a Better Relationship. It has helped me to clarify my thoughts and feelings about me, you, and us.

I have thought very carefully about our relationship, and I have decided that I do not want things to change: that is, I want to continue doing all that we have been doing in my relationship with you.

I have searched my heart and my soul, and I believe this is the best course of action for me to take in my life right now.

I recognize that by doing 'more of the same', we are almost certainly likely to achieve the same results as we have in the past... and that our relationship will continue to be very much like it is now.

This is what I truly want.

Sincerely and lovingly,

_____ (Sign it with your first name)

Date_____

POSSIBILITY #2: MAKE CHANGES TO IMPROVE THE RELATIONSHIP

If your decision is to stay in the relationship and work to make it better, we suggest you write out a declaration similar to the one below. Use this as a template to create your own declaration. It is important to carefully reflect on all the implications of your choice.

Dear .... (Your partner's name, or Hi Sweetie, or whatever your own term of endearment may be),

As you know, I have been reading a book <u>8 Weeks to a Better Relationship</u>. It has helped me to clarify my thoughts and feelings about me, you, and us. I have thought very carefully about our relationship, and I have decided to make a commitment to invest my time, energy, passion and love to improve my relationship with you.

I have searched my heart and my soul, and I believe this is an important and necessary step for me to take in my life right now.

I also recognize I will be asked to be truthful with myself and with you, to share my thoughts, ideas and feelings, to reveal who I am even though this makes me vulnerable, may cause pain, or change the way you see me. I commit to allowing you to 'see-into-me' as this is what intimacy is about.

I am open to changing my behaviors, attitudes and assump-

tions . I am open to having an entirely different relationship with you than the one we have had up to now.

I hope you share my feelings and intentions, and look forward to building a better relationship together with you.

Sincerely and lovingly,

_____ (Sign your first name)

Date _____

POSSIBILITY #3: END YOUR RELATIONSHIP

If your decision is to end your relationship with your partner, we suggest you write out a declaration similar to the one below. The importance of this declaration is to firmly identify your direction. The declaration helps you to move on. Use this as a template to create your own declaration.

Dear ………… (Your partner's name, or Hi Sweetie, or whatever your own term of endearment may be),

As you know, I have been reading the book 8 Weeks to a Better Relationship. It has helped me to clarify my thoughts and feelings about me, you, and us.

I have thought very carefully about our relationship, and it is with sadness that am writing to tell you I have made the decision to lovingly and harmoniously end my relationship with you. I have searched my heart and my soul, and I sincerely believe this is the necessary step for me to take in my life right now.

I have come to recognize—with no negative judgment—that what I desire in a relationship is significantly different from what you desire in a relationship. And so, I believe the most loving decision at this time is to release you with love, and ask you to release me with love.

I am truly grateful for the gifts and opportunities this relationship has given me. I know our relationship can end in a loving and respectful way, and that we can honor each other for the rest of our lives even if we choose not to be in a relationship the way we are now.

I recognize that endings often evoke feelings of grief and loss. I will honor my feelings of grief and loss as well as your feelings of grief and loss.

I will be as truthful with myself and with you, to share my thoughts, ideas and feelings, to reveal who I am even though this makes me vulnerable. I commit to myself and to you with respect and dignity.

I am choosing to make this change in my life and to risk having an entirely different relationship with you than I have now, because I truly believe it is in both of our best interests to do this.

Sincerely and lovingly,

---------------------------- (Sign it with your first name)

Date _____

As you read through your declaration to end your relationship, are you clear this is what you really want?

For some, this moment of contemplating the ending of their relationship helps them recognize that they really *don't* want to end their relationship.

If this is the case for you, what option do you choose now? Remember, <u>there are only three possibilities</u>, and by eliminating one, you are left with only two.

Take your time. Talk to your best friend or a trusted relative, or therapist. This is an extremely important decision; one of the most important of your entire life.

Don't rush it; but also don't delay it too long and get stuck in *'analysis paralysis'*.

But whatever you decide, *<u>make a full commitment to it</u>*.

WHAT HAPPENS IF YOUR PARTNER'S DECISION IS DIFFERENT FROM YOURS?

No matter which of the above options you have chosen—to do more of the same, to work towards improving the relationship, or deciding to release one another—there is the possibility that your partner will want to pursue a different direction.

That's what this period of sharing is all about: to share each other's thoughts and feelings, and to discuss them in a more open and honest way than ever before.

Sometimes this will result in a wonderfully close bonding; a depth in your relationship that neither of you has experienced before. Sometimes it will shock your partner to hear you express yourself from the bottom of your soul and heart, with complete honesty and without judgment for the other.

Sometimes they will get angry and fearful.

Whatever you do, and whatever they do, it is vital that you strive to stay fully in the moment, and completely avoid any references to what happened in the past.

Talk about how you feel *now*; what decision you have reached *in this moment* after a great deal of careful and loving deliberation.

At this point it serves no purpose to get angry or bitter or defensive. All that is needed is your complete honesty, whether your partner is prepared to hear that or not.

It is the ultimate expression of integrity for you to speak your truth with loving and caring intent, with compassion, and with complete transparency. Remember that you are not responsible for your partner's reactions to what you say—you are only responsible for what you say, and how you say it.

If your partner's reaction is negative, or angry, or a flood of tears, you need to strongly resist the urge to 'rescue' them.

Just know that as long as your intention is loving and altruistic, standing your ground will give you dignity and strength, and offer a solid foundation for your partner to accept and move on.

SUMMARY

At this stage you should have a clear direction for your future. You have shared your vision of your ideal relationship with your partner. You have had an opportunity to hear your partner's vision of his/her ideal relationship.

You have assessed the degree of shared overlap in your visions for a relationship, identified a clear direction to pursue, and have committed your intentions to paper.

Your final step is to share the declaration of your intentions with your partner. How and when to do this will require careful thought.

Next week we will help you and your partner develop a plan of action for your future.

PAUSE AND PONDER

➶ **What ideas stood out the most for you this week?**

➶ **What ideas were new for you?**

➶ **What ideas were challenging and difficult for you to accept or understand?**

🖎 **What did you learn about yourself?**

🖎 **What did you learn about your partner?**

CONGRATULATIONS!

You have completed **Week 6** on your journey to a Better Relationship.

WEEK 7:

Watch your thoughts; they become words.
Watch your words; they become actions.
Watch your actions; they become habits.
Watch your habits; they become character.
Watch your character; it becomes your
destiny.

(Variously attributed to Lao Tzu, Mahatma Ghandi,
Buddha, and others)

WELCOME TO WEEK SEVEN.

Last week was a very important week in your journey toward
a better relationship. You met with your partner and shared your

visions for an ideal relationship. Then you assessed the degree to which the two of you hold a similar vision. And finally, you identified a future direction and committed your intentions to paper.

The activities of Week 7 are crucial to creating a better relationship. During this week you will develop a plan of action to take you closer to your ideal relationship.

In previous weeks you identified *what* you want to experience in your relationship. This week you will answer *how*.

Answering 'how' is the second step in creating change. A 'how' question propels you into action because the answer is always action-oriented.

And even if, on your journey to a better relationship, you decide to end your current one and get ready to move on to the next, the activities of Week 7 will help you achieve a better relationship in the future.

THE ABSENCE OF 'WHY?'

You may have noticed that we've consistently avoided asking 'why' questions throughout our journey. This is because asking 'why' does not produce change.

Instead, the opposite occurs. The reason for this becomes evident when you understand the function of a 'why' question.

The function of a 'why' question is to justify or explain past behavior. Its focus is in the past; it relates to *old behavior*.

In our efforts to create a better relationship we are not interested in past behavior, only present and future behaviors. No matter what you do, you can't change a single second of what happened in the past.

The only action you can take is <u>now</u>, in this present moment. And only by taking action right now, can you influence what happens in the future.

If you are committed to making your relationship better, then we suggest you avoid asking '*Why?*'. Instead, focus upon '*What?*' and '*How?*':

"*What do I want?*" and, "*How shall I get there?*"

If you catch yourself indulging in a 'why' question, try to immediately acknowledge it and stop it. This line of questioning will only keep you going around in circles and focusing on old behavior and events. It's worth repeating: the past cannot be changed. There is no point in spending your time and energy on things that cannot be changed.

The goal of Week 7 is to develop new behaviors; to change the way you relate to your partner, and to build a better future. You do this by designing an *action plan*.

It is easier to act your way into a better mode of thinking, than to think yourself into a better mode of acting.

Lee Johnson & Albert Koopman:
How to Escape your Comfort Zones

An effective action plan answers the following questions:

1. What is your goal?

2. What are the obstacles or barriers to achieving your goal?

3. Who are your resources?

4. How will you achieve your goal?

5. What is your timeline?

6. How will you document your progress?

7. How will you celebrate your accomplishments?

When following an action plan, some people have a tendency to focus on only one or two components of the plan and ignore the others. We encourage you to follow all the steps faithfully and completely.

Experience has taught us the importance of every one of these components in designing an effective action plan.

Take the time necessary to answer all of the above questions fully by following each of these steps.

STEP ONE: IDENTIFY YOUR GOAL

The first step in designing an effective action plan is to *identify your goal*. This is where you identify what you want the outcome to look like—the end result. It is necessary to have 'the end in mind' when you begin. The work you completed in Week 2 will be relevant here.

We suggest you start with a goal that is small and achievable. As you succeed in achieving smaller goals, you build confidence and momentum to achieve larger goals.

Furthermore, when you have a clear sense of what you want to accomplish, the likelihood of achieving success is high.

In our work with couples we often ask the questions:

"How will we know when our counseling work is finished?"

or,

"How will things be when we are done?"

and,

"What will success look like?"

Answering these questions is an important step in making change. We recognize that most people initially cannot answer these questions easily.

Alice turns to the caterpillar and asks,
"Which road should I take?"
The caterpillar responds with a question of his own.
"Where are you going?"
"Well," says Alice, "I don't really know."
The caterpillar comments,
"If you don't know where you are going
then it doesn't matter which road you take, does it?

Lewis Carroll
Alice In Wonderland

PAUSE AND PONDER

Review the work you did in Week 2. What were your answers to the question "What does your ideal relationship look like?"

Using this information, identify <u>one specific behavior</u> that will move you closer to your ideal relationship. Write this in the space below as a goal.

✎ **One small, achievable goal I want to work on is:**

To help you, here are some examples of achievable goals:

- Spend 30 minutes of quality time with my partner each day

- Take a 15 minute walk with my partner each day

- Kiss my partner goodbye in the morning and greet my partner hello in the evening

- Make love to my partner at least 2 times per week

- Dedicate one evening a week to do something fun and interesting with my partner, other than watch TV

- Reveal at least one of my thoughts and feelings to my partner every day

- Ask my partner about their day, and listen fully to their answer

- Hug my partner each morning, and express my gratitude for having him or her in my life

Even if you are planning to end your present relationship, identify some behaviors that might serve you well in a future relationship. Behaviors like:

- Clearly ask for what I want from others

- Take 30 minutes of time for me each day

- Make my expectations clear and explicit

- Express my intentions with three 'I' messages daily

Remember: *a goal without specifics is just a dream.* And so, when identifying a goal, make sure it meets all of the following criteria:

- Measurable
- Specific

- Positive

- Concrete

- Attainable

By *measurable*, we mean you must be able to measure whether you have attained your goal or not. A good way to test if you have selected a measurable goal is to ask yourself the question, *"Can someone else determine if I have been successful in attaining my goal?"* If someone other than yourself can measure your success, then it is likely you have selected a measurable goal.

By *specific*, your goal should answer the *Who, What, Where, When,* and *How* questions: Who is involved? What exactly do I want to accomplish? Where do I want to do this? When will this happen—i.e. what is my time frame for achieving this? How exactly will I do it? (You should also identify the requirements and constraints).

Finally, you should have a specific reason; an ultimate purpose in wishing to accomplish the goal. This is the passion that fuels the engine.

Example of a vague or general goal: *"I want to get in shape."* But a specific goal would be, *"I am going to join the gym at the Community Center today and commit to working out four days a week."*

By *positive*, we mean that your goal should enhance your life and make things better, easier, more pleasant, more exciting, more harmonious, or whatever other positive outcomes you can think of.

Below are examples of goals that do and do not meet the required criteria, and the reason:

"I will be happier." (Not measurable—rather write something like, *"I will make a list of positive affirmations and read them out loud every morning."*)

"My partner will be happier." (Not measurable, and also something you can't control—rather focus on your own actions and write something like, *"I will offer my partner at least one sincere compliment every day."*)

"There is no more fighting or yelling." (Negative focus— also, remember you can only control what you do, so rather write something like, *"I will be conscious of taking full responsibility for my emotions if we disagree, and if necessary I will count slowly to ten or ask for a time-out."*)

"There will be no more affairs." (Negative focus— again, remember you can only control what you do… so, rather write something like, *"I will be completely monogamous in my relationship. I will nurture my commitment to my partner daily by being open and honest with my thoughts and feelings. Should I have thoughts of investing my emotional energy in another person or activity, I will disclose these thoughts to my partner."*)

"Less TV watching." (Not specific enough—rather write something like, *"I will limit my TV watching to no more than one hour daily."*)

"More sex." (Not specific enough—rather write something like, *"I will initiate sexual contact with my partner at least once a week."*)

"Better time together." (Not concrete enough—rather write something like, *"I will plan at least one date a week in some interesting place—a walk in the park, a picnic on the beach, reading a book on the river bank, strolling through the forest—so that we can have an opportunity to talk while being stimulated by new things."*)

"More peace." (Not concrete enough—rather write something like, *"I will commit to 30 minutes of meditation at least three times a week."*)

Note that while each of the original statements is a legitimate goal, all fail to meet one or more of the criteria of being specific, positive, concrete, measurable or attainable.

So, take a look at the goal you wrote down in the space above and make sure it meets these criteria.

If it doesn't, you will need to rework it in the same way as our suggestions in the examples above.

STEP TWO: IDENTIFY OBSTACLES

The second step towards developing an effective action plan, is to *identify obstacles or barriers to achieving your goal.*

Don't assume there are no obstacles. If your goal were easy to accomplish, you would have achieved it already!

One way to identify your obstacles is to ask yourself the question, *"What has prevented me from achieving this goal so far?"* There is a tendency to skim over this step. Don't! Only by identifying and addressing specific obstacles, can they be addressed and overcome.

To help you identify your own obstacles, we offer a description of some that we've frequently observed in relationships:

1. **Fear**

2. **Focusing on the past**

3. **Giving away responsibility**

4. **Believing there is 'no choice'**

5. **Blame**

6. **Right/wrong thinking**

7. **Attachments**

8. **Belief in not enough**

9. **Needing to look good**

10. **Anger and resentment**

The following is a brief description of some of these obstacles. Read them carefully and try to identify those that may prevent you from achieving your goal of a better relationship.

FEAR

Fear is one of the biggest obstacles to creating a better relationship—fear of what might happen if you change your way of behaving; fear of the unknown; and fear of rejection; fear of disappointment or failure.

If you want to create a better relationship it is essential that you address your fears and develop a strategy to overcome them.

Fear can be very powerful. It can paralyze you and stop you from taking actions that might be good for you. To help you face up to your fears and overcome them, here are some suggestions:

Are you aware that fear is always about the _future_? Fear is created in your mind whenever you imagine a negative outcome in the future.

Fear is never about a _present_ experience. Think of a time when you felt afraid. Was the fear due to something you were experiencing at that very moment or were you thinking ahead, beyond the present moment and imagining a negative outcome?

Consider this example: Have you ever had the opportunity to speak in public? Did you notice any anxiety in anticipation of giving your speech? Did you also notice that the anxiety virtually disappeared once you began to speak?

This is because anxiety and fear is always the result of *imagining a negative outcome in the future.* Here's a good way of remembering it:

FEAR = Future Events Appearing Real

One way of overcoming fear is by acknowledging that it is an imaginary scenario that you create; a picture that you have painted of a negative outcome.

Once you train yourself to notice that this is what you are doing, bring your attention back into the present moment. Look around you.

Almost magically, you will find your fear has diminished.

The feeling of anxiety is your body's way of warning you that your head (mind) has become 'disconnected' from your body. Your body creates anxiety as a way of signaling that your mind is somewhere other than where your body is at that specific moment. When you reconnect your head with your body, your anxiety will dissipate. Try it and see for yourself.

We will have more to say about fear in Week 8, but think about this in the meantime:

Even if there were a ravenous tiger that has just escaped from a zoo and is about to attack you, your feelings of fear are based on your collective knowledge of how dangerous tigers are, and stories of people who have been attacked by tigers. If a small child encounters a snake, there is no fear if there is no frame of reference for fearing it.

FOCUSING ON THE PAST

A second obstacle people have when attempting to behave in new ways is the tendency to *focus on the past.*

Many couples become stuck by continuing to be 'chained' to past experiences, rather than placing their focus on the present and future.

In our experience, many couples will focus almost entirely upon the past during their initial session of counseling. Often therapists are partially responsible by asking questions as, "*Why are you here?*"

Often their intention is merely to get background information and understand the situation, but couples sometimes respond by trying to justify their own position or blame their partner. We believe a better question is, "*What do you want to create in your relationship now?*"

Most people believe they need to understand old behavior before they can create new behaviors. While understanding may be helpful, it is not necessary.

We've learned to be cautious about focusing upon the past. We believe placing one's attention on the past is about as effective as driving a car by looking through the rear view mirror.

You cannot move forward while chained to events and issues of the past.

Our strategy is to <u>release the past</u>, <u>embrace the present</u>, and <u>create the future</u>.

GIVING AWAY RESPONSIBILITY

A third obstacle to effective change is to give away the responsibility for creating the change.

Many people are unable to move forward because they want someone else—typically their partner—to change first. By insisting that others change first, they effectively give away their power and make someone else responsible for creating change.

It's not uncommon to hear one partner in a relationship say, *"I'll be happy when my partner does..."*.

Whenever you make a statement such as this, you are giving away your responsibility for creating the change you desire. And when you give away your responsibility, you give away your power. You cannot create change in your relationship if you are acting as though you are powerless.

When you focus on what is within *your power to change*, you are creating an action plan that is possible. If you focus on what your partner needs to change, you are expecting action that is not within your power to make happen.

Effective change is possible when you take responsibility for things over which you have control, and refuse to take responsibility for things over which you have no control.

BELIEVING YOU HAVE 'NO CHOICE'

We introduced this concept in detail in Week 1. Failure to acknowledge choice is a major barrier to achieving a goal. If you believe you have 'no choice', yet continue to behave in ways that you always have, you will get the same results. An action plan is based on the premise that you <u>do</u> have choice. In fact, you have a number of options to consider.

It is your responsibility to choose the option that you believe will achieve your desired goal. Many people continue doing more of the same because they have consciously or unconsciously limited the kinds of options they can access.

In order to achieve your goal of a better relationship, you have to open yourself up to new possibilities, new behaviors, and new ways of living. We remind you of the quotation from Week 1 :

Unless you change your direction
you will end up where you are headed.
If nothing changes, nothing changes.

Pay attention to your thoughts. If you hear yourself say, "*I have no choice...*", you are creating a barrier to achieving your goals. Remember that you <u>always</u> have a choice, and that choice can be exercised right now, in this moment. You can activate your power anytime you want to.

BLAME

Blame is another way of focusing on behavior other than your own. It is just another way of giving away responsibility for achieving your goal; it is about giving someone else (or something else) the power to prevent you from taking responsibility and moving ahead.

Blame is also about being focused on the past rather than the present. To be effective in creating change, you need to keep your focus on the present. Focus on what it is <u>you</u> can do differently. Blame will increase your emotions of anger and frustration without contributing anything constructive to making change.

Observe, identify choices, and then decide.

There is little benefit to be derived from blaming others—or even yourself. Rather than continuing to beat yourself up, ask what positive lessons you have learned from your experiences. Recognize that at the time, you made the best decision that was available at that time. Now, move on.

6. RIGHT/WRONG THINKING

Right/wrong thinking is actually not thinking. When you see the world purely from the perspective of 'right/wrong', you are not engaging your intellect. Instead you may be doing what author Ray Woollam describes as 'bin-ing'.

Woollam says that most of us 'bin' or categorize our thoughts, events, or experiences as 'good' or 'bad', 'right' or 'wrong', or various other labels that have the same effect—limiting our perspective to simplistic, black and white thinking.

The danger of this kind of automatic categorization is that you may mistakenly believe you are thinking, when actually you are not. Thinking is about weighing, considering, evaluating, and deciding. Typically, once you've 'binned' something, you have a tendency to stop thinking about whatever it is you have 'binned'. For most, once you've put it into its proper container, the thinking, weighing, considering, or deciding stops.

The world is too complex to categorize all events, ideas, or experiences as only right/wrong or good/bad. This is also true in relationships. Often when people have been together for some time, they stop being fully engaged in the moment and go into 'auto-pilot mode' when their partner does something or makes a comment.

We do our partner and ourselves a disservice when we 'bin' their thoughts, feelings, and/or behaviors as either 'good' or 'bad' or 'right' or 'wrong'.

You might ask, "*What is the alternative to bin-ing?*"

One option is to suspend right/wrong bin-ing as often as possible and stay fully present, opening up your mind to each idea, event, and experience. Be receptive to allowing your ideas about life to be modified by others. Replace the language of bin-ing (right/wrong) with the language of 'difference' ("*Ahhh, that's different.*")

Honor and celebrate differences. Enjoy the richness of life.

Out beyond ideas of wrong-doing and right-doing
there is a field.
I'll meet you there.

Rumi

7. ATTACHMENTS

Another obstacle to achieving a goal is our attachment to things, beliefs, objects, or people. Tanis Helliwell, author of *Take Your Soul to Work*, describes three kinds of relationships: *Cohesive*, *Adhesive*, and *Repulsive*.

Of course, not all relationships fit neatly into these categories, but try to determine where your relationship is most similar.

A *Cohesive* relationship is where two people together become more than they were individually. It's 1+1 = 3. Through their relationship, they help one another change and grow and become better overall than they were prior to the relationship.

An *Adhesive* relationship is where people are stuck together and resist growing (themselves or their partner) out of fear they might become 'unstuck'.

Their goal is not growth/development/enrichment, but simply staying together.

A *Repulsive* relationship is one where individuals destroy each other through the relationship. A physically, emotionally, psychologically, or sexually abusive relationship is an example of a repulsive relationship.

Disconnecting from an adhesive relationship often causes immense pain. We have worked with many people who are too closely attached to their mates, children, jobs, house, car, status, job title, or a belief system (to name a few common objects of attachment).

There is nothing wrong with feeling and expressing great

love, but if you experience intense emotional pain when disconnecting from something, it may be an indication of being overly attached.

It is important to be aware of your attachments—and if your attachments are not congruent with your goals, they can be a huge barrier to achieving growth.

We're not suggesting you be heartless or emotionally detached. Instead, we're suggesting you cultivate a healthy sense of self, and a proper perspective on your relationship to other people and things and environments.

Enjoy and appreciate, but do not become <u>attached</u> to it.

8. AN ATTITUDE OF SCARCITY

A belief in *scarcity* is a common barrier to creating change in relationships. Some people explain that the reason they can't change, is because they don't have enough time or money or energy. They act as if this condition is out of their control.

This is another example of not taking responsibility for one's own life. By using excuses such as *not enough time, money,* or *energy* we are saying we are not responsible for our life as it is.

The truth is that claiming *not enough* of anything is a way of saying 'no' without taking responsibility for the decision. When somebody says they don't have the time, energy, or money to do something, what they are really saying is, "*I don't choose to use the time, energy, or money I have for this purpose.*"

We have met many couples who claimed they didn't have enough time to talk to each other, yet seemed to find plenty of time to go shopping or watch their favorite TV program.

Others claimed to not have enough money to attend counseling, yet could always find money for a few beers after work, a round of golf, or that new couch that was on sale.

'Not enough' is often a way of not taking responsibility.

Of course, there are circumstances that contribute to a *less than enough* situation—for example, when the world has been struggling through some pretty rough economic times and people have lost their jobs, their pensions, and their homes, it's easy to blame the 'not enough' on external circumstances, people and events. And yet, you still have the power of choice every single moment of your life: the power to make a decision to do something about it.

History is filled with stories of people who have lost everything, and yet risen to great success and prosperity and happiness. Often they will look back and say that it was in fact those dire circumstances that were the catalyst for their success.

9. WANTING TO LOOK GOOD TO OTHERS

For some people, wanting to look good for others gets in the way of creating effective change in their relationship. The need to 'look good' allows others to have power over us.

When we make decisions based upon *how others see us* rather than what works for us, we tend not to choose wisely. Egoism affects our ability to choose wisely.

Take charge of your emotional well-being and sense of worth. Make <u>yourself</u> the person responsible for determining your worth. Don't give this responsibility away to others.

There is a wise saying which may help those who are easily affected by what others think about us: "*What other people think about me is none of my business.*"

Become less invested in what others think and say about you. Become invested in making decisions based upon what <u>you</u> think about you.

10. ANGER AND RESENTMENT

Anger and resentment are indications of being focused on the past. Anger is always about the past; about *old stories.*

Anger weighs you down and impedes your ability to move forward.

When you think about it, anger and resentment are negative energies that gnaw away at you day after day—often without the person you are angry at, even being aware of it.

It does far more harm to *you* than the person towards whom your anger is directed.

If you want to be happy, joyful, and peaceful, it is imperative that you spend most of your waking hours in the present. Let go of the past; truly forgive and release. By doing so, you will release the power that the past event (or person) still has over you.

Remember, *you* have given these events or people permission to have power over you by continuing to invest emotional energy (anger) in the past.

Forgiveness is giving up all hope
of a better past.

Lily Tomlin

PAUSE AND PONDER

Reflect upon the obstacles in your life. Identify what has prevented you from achieving your goals in the past. What are you allowing to get in your way now?

List these obstacles and how they impact your life.

This is an important exercise because these obstacles have stopped you in the past—and you want the outcome to be different this time.

⤳ My Obstacles Are:

My Obstacles Are (continued):

STEP THREE: IDENTIFY RESOURCES

Challenges are never easy, but the challenges of life can more easily be managed with good resources. Andrew Carnegie, once the richest man in the world, had a strategy of always surrounding himself with resourceful people. He knew that he could accomplish more things more easily if he asked others to help him.

Who are the people who, if asked, might help you achieve your goals? Who might support you in creating a better relationship in your life?

Some of these are people around you right now—your partner, family members, friends, and colleagues. Others are people you may need to invite into your life—like a therapist, a spiritual advisor, or a mentor.

The key to having people as resources is to ask for their assistance. Most people will be pleased to help you achieve your goals. But they will become resources only if you invite them.

The more people you invite into your life, the easier your challenges become. The expression, *Many hands make light work* is based upon multiplying resources of wisdom and life experience. By asking for help, you bring more resources to you.

Asking for help also forces you to declare your intentions publicly. The act of making a public declaration is a powerful form of encouragement and reinforcement. You are much more likely to stick to your action plan if you have declared your goals out loud and have others with you on your journey. A silent, isolated individual is usually less likely to succeed.

The founders of Alcoholics Anonymous understood the importance of developing resources when making a change, and also the power of declaring your status out loud: "*I am John, and I am an alcoholic.*"

Each individual in A.A. has a sponsor or a resource person. They know that asking for help, and being open to receiving help, is essential to achieving a successful outcome.

PAUSE AND PONDER

➳ **My present resources are:**

➳ **These people might help me if I ask them:**

STEP FOUR: IDENTIFY A STRATEGY

This is the most important component of your action plan. This is where you identify the *specific behaviors you will take to achieve your goal.*

Your strategy needs to include ways you intend to address the obstacles you've identified above. It is important that your strategy is *clear, specific, concrete,* and *measurable.*

We've also learned that creating an action plan requires asking the right questions.

THE IMPORTANCE OF ASKING THE RIGHT QUESTION

In order to be successful, you need to ask the following questions:

1. **What?**
2. **How?**
3. **Who?**
4. **When?**
5. **Where?**

By asking 'what', you create a *list of information.*

By asking 'how', you identify the method or *strategy for achieving your goal.*

By asking 'who', you identify the *names of specific individuals.*

By asking 'when', you identify a *particular time or deadline.*

And finally, by asking 'where', you identify a *location.*

This information is summarized below:

Type of Question	Function
What	List of information
How	Action
Who	Name
When	Time
Where	Location

The answers to each of these questions contribute to identifying the specific information you require to develop your strategy. We invite you to take time now to answer each of these questions. A sample action plan has also been provided to guide you.

WHAT?

What are the exact behaviors you need to do to achieve your goal? List these on pages 286 and 287.

One way to assist you to identify the exact behaviors or activities is to list them under the following categories.

Ask yourself:

What behaviors do I want to:

       ≈> **Keep?**   (= maintain)

       ≈> **Stop?**   (= let go of)

       ≈> **Start?** (= initiate)

KEEP

What behaviors and activities do you want to keep; to maintain; and do more of? What behaviors and activities are you happy with? What things do you or your partner currently do which, if continued, would contribute to your goal?

These are the behaviors you want to keep.

To maintain a healthy relationship it is important to recognize the behaviors that contribute to the well-being of your relationship. By making a list of behaviors to be maintained, each person feels acknowledged and motivated to keep up the good work.

It is just as important to acknowledge and praise desirable behaviors, as it is to identify the undesirable ones.

STOP

What behaviors and activities do you want to stop, let go of, and do less of? Which behaviors and activities cause you pain? Which take you and your relationship in the wrong direction?

What actions or behaviors will improve the quality of your relationship if you stop doing them? Stopping destructive behaviors is just as important as starting new constructive behaviors.

START

What new behaviors and activities do you want to start, initiate, and do in your relationship now? What new actions will contribute toward achieving your goal of a better relationship? What behaviors need to be initiated to address the obstacles and barriers identified above?

WRITE:

✎ **List your 'Keep', 'Stop', and 'Start' behaviors and activities below**:

✎ **Keep:**

∝⇔ **Stop:**

∝⇔ **Start:**

☯

HOW?

The answer to 'How?' identifies the specific strategies needed to achieve the goals you have listed above. For example, if you identified that you intend to buy flowers for your partner once a week, then answering 'how' fills in the details. The 'how' might be "*I will stop at the Quickie Mart on the corner of 1st and Kingsway on my way home from work every Friday afternoon.*"

A good answer to a 'How?' question will also answer the following questions—who, when, and where. In the above example the answer to 'Who?' is 'I'. "*I will stop at the Quickie Mart.*" The answer to 'When?' is: "*On Friday afternoon on my way home from work*". And the answer to 'Where?' is, "*The Quickie Mart on the corner of 1st Avenue and Kingsway*".

Your answer to 'How?' needs to address all of the variables listed above. If one of your obstacles is 'not enough time', how you will prioritize the time to complete the desired behavior? Use the sample below as a guide to creating your action plan.

WRITE:

⟾ **My goal is (What?):**

➵ **My strategy to achieve this goal is:**

➵ **How?**

➵ **Who?**

➵ **When?**

➵ **Where?**

STEP FIVE: IDENTIFY A TIMELINE

An important component that many people disregard when creating an action plan, is to identify a *specific timeline* for achieving your goals. When will you begin your plan? What length of time do you anticipate to achieve your goals?

With some goals, the timeline will be self-evident. For example, if your goal is to kiss your partner goodbye in the morning, you can start immediately. However, a goal to stop smoking may require more consideration. You might decide to stop suddenly, or decide to gradually reduce smoking over a period of time. Or you may make an appointment to see a specialist who can help you stop; or sign up for a program or product online.

Whatever your goal, it's important to identify a timeline suited to the goal you have chosen. Setting a time is like putting a stake in the ground.

STEP SIX: IDENTIFY HOW TO DOCUMENT YOUR PROGRESS

Documenting your progress is another component of an action plan. This is important to maintain the focus on your goals and to monitor your progress in achieving them.

By documenting your progress, you receive the necessary feedback as to whether your action plan is working or not. Documenting your progress also helps ensure you have selected a goal that is clear, specific, concrete, measurable and attainable.

Typical documentation requires that you make a record of each time the desired behavior or action has occurred or not occurred. This provides valuable information to confirm if you are on track or not, or to indicate that you need to redesign your action plan.

Many plans initially fail because they do not take into consideration all of the obstacles to a successful outcome. By carefully monitoring your progress, you are able to recognize early whether your strategy is working or not.

WRITE:

✎> **My method of documentation will be:**

(Examples: A notepad and pen next to my bed, which I will fill in every night before turning out the light. A file on my computer, which I will add to first thing in the morning when I get to work. A calendar on my refrigerator, which I will mark daily when I achieve my goal).

Celebrating your success is an important part of an action plan. Events or rituals that honor your hard work and progress are necessary to affirm the changes you have made. When you celebrate your success, you declare these changes out loud. You reinforce the changes by associating success with pleasure.

We encourage you to organize an event to celebrate your success. Invite all the people who have been your resources. Don't be shy. Honor and celebrate your good work.

PROGRESS, NOT PERFECTION

These are the components of an effective action plan. By completing the tasks identified this week, you move in the direction of positive change in your relationship. Your goal here is progress, not perfection.

Don't expect to accomplish everything overnight. Mark Twain wrote, "*The longest journey begins with an initial step*". That's all it takes: one small action each day.

The bottom line is that to create a better relationship in your life, it is essential that you take action. Action is the core ingredient in *8 Weeks to a Better Relationship*. Action is the only way you will improve your relationship. Action begins <u>now</u>. (In Week 8 we will also help you review your progress, identify new obstacles, and inspire you to maintain your progress.)

On the following page is a template you can use to create your action plan. Use the headings on this page to help you create your own action plan for achieving all of your goals.

(You can also download a PDF of a blank template on our website http://www.8weekstoabetterrelationship.com).

Then, once you have completed your action plan, tape it to your bathroom mirror, refrigerator, date book, or other visible location.

SAMPLE ACTION PLAN
(use this as a guide to creating your own)

⤳ My ideal Relationship is:

I desire a relationship where there is ease, calm, peacefulness, respect, and dignity for one another.... one where there is a high degree of communication, sharing, and touch. A relationship where there is a commitment to always tell the truth, to be completely transparent in thoughts and actions, and to be open and honest with one another.

⤳ My Goal

My goal is to increase the amount of sharing in my relationship. My specific goal is to engage in a daily period of sharing with my partner for a minimum of 15 minutes, five out of seven days per week. My desire is to express my thoughts and feelings and to create an opportunity to hear my partner's thoughts and feelings.

⤳ Obstacles

Obstacles that could prevent me from achieving my goal are:

- Too tired.
- Not enough time.
- Feeling distant.
- Fear of being vulnerable and transparent.
- No privacy.

⤳ Resources

Resources that could help me achieve my goal are:

- Children.
- Susan —family friend.
- My Parents.
- Neighbors Jenny and Andy.

⤳ Timeline

I am starting today—right now, in fact.

⤳ Documentation

 294

On the calendar on my refrigerator, I will record the days and events that help me move closer towards achieving my goal. I will mark those successes with a happy face. If I feel I have failed to take the actions necessary to achieve my goals, I will mark that with a sad face.

⤳ Strategic Plan

I will facilitate this sharing by utilizing an exercise called 'High - Low'. With this exercise I will share with my partner the high point of my day and the low point of my day.

Once I have shared my high and low points with my partner, I will invite my partner to do the same. I must remind myself that there will be no need to discuss this sharing in detail, or to try to resolve any challenges I or my partner might identify.

The only goal will be to share my thoughts and feelings with my partner, and vice versa.

Who:	My partner and I.
Where:	Lying in bed together.
When:	Last thing in the evening; we agree to set this time so that we can do this.
How:	I will share my high and low points, and then invite my partner to do the same. Afterwards I will thank my partner for sharing with me.

I will commit to this exercise regardless of how tired I

am, or how tough or busy my day has been. I will allow the sharing to be brief if I or my partner feels tired or anxious, but will not use these emotions as an excuse not to share. My priority is to build a better relationship.

(Authors' Note: The exercise can be short or long, depending upon time and energy. Also, it's a good idea to choose a time when you will not feel rushed or anxious. With regard to the above exercise, both partners are 'morning people' and so first thing in the morning works for them.

You might want to do it at night before bedtime, if that works better for both of you. You may also want to share your goals with your children and invite their support {depending on their age, and with your partner's agreement, of course}.

It may be workable to do the sharing at the dinner table with everyone there.)

⇜ Celebration

I will celebrate each success with a treat of a large slice of cheesecake.

MY OWN ACTION PLAN:

🔖 **Goal**

🔖 **Obstacles**

🔖 **Resources**

➤ **Timeline**

➤ **Documentation**

➤ **Strategic Plan**

Who:

Where:

When:

How:

⤜➤ **Celebration**

PAUSE AND PONDER

⤜➤ **What ideas stood out the most for you this week?**

⤜➤ **What ideas were new for you?**

299

☞ **What ideas were challenging and difficult for you to accept or understand?**

☞ **What did you learn about yourself?**

✍ **What did you learn about your partner?**

CONGRATULATIONS!

You have completed **Week** 7 on your journey to a better relationship.

≋WEEK 8:

*Follow your bliss and doors will open
where there were no doors before.*

Joseph Campbell

Welcome to week eight.

This is our final week together on your journey to a better relationship.

Last week you selected an initial goal and designed a specific plan of action to achieve your goal. Our focus this week is to encourage and inspire you to continue on this path of change. We also intend to provide you with a number of tools to help you maintain your commitment to a better relationship.

THE CHALLENGE OF CHANGE

Change can be difficult for most people. We know that even though many will experience the joy of an improved relationship over these eight weeks, it is not uncommon to slip back into old ways of behaving.

You might even stop doing the things that are working to improve your relationship.

This is just human nature. It's not uncommon for people to assume that once they experience an improvement, they can discontinue the behaviors that contributed to the improvement. It's not unlike having successfully dieted and lost weight, and then returning to the eating patterns that contributed to weight gain in the first place.

Fortunately you don't need to understand why this occurs to be successful in maintaining change. You only need to recognize the tendency to return to old ways of behaving, and continually recommit yourself to your goal of making your relationship better.

THE PATH OF CHANGE

In our experience, change is like deciding to walk a new path. Whenever we start down a new path it feels strange and unfamiliar. We may even experience some fear due to the uncertainty of where this new path might take us.

Sometimes, because of our fear and unease, we return to an

old and familiar path. The problem is, while the old path would feel familiar and comfortable, it might be taking us in a direction we no longer wish to go.

If you are feeling some discomfort on your new path, this might simply be confirmation that you *are* on a new path. As a matter of fact, if you do not experience some feelings of newness and unfamiliarity, it's possible that you are still on the old path.

Change requires that we have courage to push beyond these feelings of unfamiliarity and continue with a new behavior until it becomes familiar. Courage doesn't mean we don't experience fear. Rather, courage is *when we continue to act in spite of our fear.*

Risk

To laugh is to risk appearing the fool.
To reach out to another is to risk involvement.
To expose feelings is to risk showing your true self.
To place your ideas and dreams before the crowd
is to risk being called naive.
To love is to risk not being loved in return.
To live is to risk dying.
To hope is to risk despair.
To try is to risk failure.

But risks must be taken because the greatest risk in life
is to risk nothing.
The people who risk nothing

Do nothing,
Have nothing,
Are nothing, and
Become nothing.

They may avoid suffering and sorrow,
but they simply cannot learn to feel,
and change, and grow, and love, and live.
Chained by their servitude they are slaves.
They have forfeited their freedom.

Only the people who risk are truly free!

Author Unknown

BUILDING TRUST

One way to develop courage is to increase your sense of trust. This could be trust in yourself, but also trust in others, trust in the universe, or trust in a higher power. An ancient ritual for developing trust was the walking of a labyrinth.

(Some people think a labyrinth is the same as a maze. In fact, it's almost the opposite[5]).

Labyrinths have been known to exist for more than 4,000 years. A labyrinth may look like a maze, with the exception

---

5   From Wikipedia: "In colloquial English, labyrinth is generally synonymous with maze, but many contemporary scholars observe a distinction between the two: maze refers to a complex branching (multicursal) puzzle with choices of path and direction; while a single-path (unicursal) labyrinth has only a single, non-branching path, which leads to the center. A labyrinth in this sense has an unambiguous route to the center and back and is not designed to be difficult to navigate."

that in a labyrinth there are no dead-ends, no detours, and no obstacles to overcome or solve. *There is only a single path.* Since there is only one path, your destination is assured.

The process of walking a labyrinth is simple. It requires setting one foot in front of the other, and trusting completely that the path will take you where you need to go. Try it for yourself, using your finger or a pencil.

A labyrinth can be a metaphor for a way of living. When someone trusts the path they are on, they move out of their mind where anxiety and fear reign and into their body where they experience peace, joy and happiness.

You may want to see if there is a labyrinth somewhere nearby, and walk it regularly as a way of reminding yourself to trust your path in life. You might even consider constructing your own labyrinth. Melissa Gayle West has written a guide for constructing a labyrinth called, *Exploring the Labyrinth: A Guide for Healing and Spiritual Growth*. Whatever means you use, developing trust in your journey is important to maintaining your commitment to your action plan.

ANOTHER WAY OF BUILDING TRUST

Another way to develop courage and trust, is to set yourself small goals that are quick and simple to achieve. Then, celebrate each time you achieve one. In this way, you will learn to trust yourself, and grow confidence in your ability to perform and achieve. As you feel yourself making progress, you may want to change it up and start setting more difficult goals.

WHAT DOES CHANGE LOOK LIKE?

Many people become discouraged when attempting to make a change because the process doesn't seem to proceed as they expected. Also, while it's common to think that change will continue as a steady progression of improvement, it usually doesn't happen that way.

In fact, it's often a stop-and-start process; sometimes taking one step forward and then two backwards, and then three forward again.

When people find themselves temporarily losing ground or

returning to old behaviors, they can become disillusioned and discouraged, and many lose faith in their action plan. Yet, it's not uncommon to return briefly to old behaviors as we endeavor to master new ones.

We prefer to describe these episodes of stepping back into old behaviors as *'doing research'*. We believe as people make significant changes in their life it is wise to collect information on their new behaviors. It is just as important to collect information on the *old* behaviors. And so, when a person repeats an old behavior we consider this part of the 'research process'.

The purpose of this phase is to remind ourselves of the reasons *why* we decided to make a change. We believe when people have collected enough information, they are able to make the necessary changes in their life.

With this in mind, we believe there are no backward steps: this 'back-stepping' behavior is actually an important component of the change process.

FALLING INTO AN OPEN SERVICE HOLE

We often use the following story to explain the process of change:

> *"Change is like walking down a street. At the end of the street there is a service hole (manhole). The cover has been removed and there is now only an open hole. Unfortunately, as you are walking down the street you fail to notice the*

309 ☯

cover has been removed… and you fall into the hole.

"You climb out of the hole, brush yourself off, and continue on your way.

"The next day you walk down the same street. Once again the cover is off the service hole. Again you fail to notice the cover has been removed, and again you fall into the hole. You climb out of the hole, brush yourself off, and continue on your way.

"On the third day, you walk down the same street. Again the cover has been removed. This time you notice the cover is off, however not soon enough to avoid falling into the hole. You climb out of the hole, brush yourself off, and continue on your way.

"On day four, you walk down the same street. This time you notice that the cover has been removed from the service hole. You step around the hole and continue on your way.

"On day five you walk down a different street!"

Change is like that. After a great deal of work and struggle, you eventually notice where the 'holes' are in your life, and you learn to walk around them. Eventually you walk down a different path and don't experience the holes at all.

All growth and progress requires change. Also, change doesn't happen all at once. It happens gradually. Change is a process of evolution. To be successful in making changes in your relationship, you need to have patience for the time it takes to learn and integrate new behaviors.

THE RIGHT ANSWER

Many people who are seeing a therapist for the first time, are surprised to learn that they do more talking than the therapist. They seem to just be answering endless questions. In fact, clients often get impatient and bluntly ask their therapists to give them the solution; the 'right answer' to solve a problem, and save them the time and the pain.

Unfortunately, nobody can 'fix' you. A therapist can't give you a pill that will magically take away your problems.

And so, whenever we are asked for 'the right answer', our response is, "*The right answer is the one that works for you.*"

It's also unfortunately impossible to know the 'right answer' ahead of time. You can only know the right answer once you have done the work and actually achieved the results you desire.

It's the same with fixing relationship problems. While it may be possible to take note of what has been the 'right' answer for others, this may or may not be the right answer for you and your partner.

You need to pay attention to the results of your behaviors, and to notice which behaviors move you closer to your goal, and which behaviors move you further away from your goal.

Using this information, you can discontinue behaviors that

don't work, and recommit yourself to behaving in ways that take you in the direction you wish to go.

The discouragement you may feel when old behaviors show up—in yourself or your partner—is often the result of judging yourself or your partner too harshly. Effective change requires encouragement, not discouragement.

Author Julia Cameron in her book, *The Artist's Way*, describes each of us as a small child who needs to be gently supported, nurtured and encouraged to grow.

Speaking harshly or being impatient with your child-self will impede your change and growth. So, be gentle with yourself as you make changes in your relationship.

TOOLS FOR CHANGE

On the next few pages we provide you with a number of tools to assist you in improving your relationship. Some tools may work better for you than others. The key to successful change is to have a large number of tools in your toolbox.

TOOL #1: TELL YOUR TRUTH

To succeed in making your relationship better, you will need to keep telling yourself and your partner the truth. *Truth telling is absolutely critical to creating a better relationship.*

And you will need to tell your truth every day.

You can't stop telling the truth once you achieve some of the

 312

results you desire. It is important to build into your relationship regular opportunities to tell your partner the truth about what you are experiencing in the relationship.

We suggest you make time on a regular basis to share all your thoughts and feelings with each other.

We have emphasized over and over again the importance of telling your truth and revealing who you are in order to experience *in-to-me-see* in your relationship. Below are some ideas of what you might share with your partner.

- What you are feeling.
- What is working for you.
- What isn't working for you.
- Your hopes and dreams for the future.
- Expression of gratitude for the relationship.
- Assessment of the closeness or distance in the relationship.
- Experiences you had recently that you liked.
- Experiences you had recently that you didn't like.
- Times when you felt annoyed, hurt, sad or disappointed.
- Times when you felt happy, grateful, peaceful and happy.

TOOL #2: HIGH – LOW

You might recall the exercise we described earlier called 'High-Low'. This exercise creates an opportunity to share the high and low points of your day.

To complete the exercise, simply share that aspect of your day that you experienced as the high point. Then share the aspect of your day that you experienced as the low point. Invite your partner to share his or her high and low points with you.

Don't examine these experiences in detail or try to solve them in any way. This is not the point of this exercise. This is merely an opportunity for sharing with one another and revealing who you are today.

TOOL #3: THE RELATIONSHIP BAROMETER

Another tool to assist you in revealing yourself to your partner is the Relationship Barometer. The barometer is a way of indicating your experience of closeness or distance in the relationship. This tool provides an easy opportunity to communicate information to your partner about the nature of your relationship. It lets you be clear and transparent with your partner, and makes it more difficult to hide behind a mask or conceal anything.

One of the interesting discoveries in using this tool is that the two of you may experience a different degree of closeness or distance at the same time.

Directions: Make a Relationship Barometer similar to the one in the diagram below. For the fingers (indicators), use a magnet or sticky note. Write your own name and your partner's name on the side. Place the Relationship Barometer on your refrigerator, bathroom mirror or other location that is visible to both you and your partner.

RELATIONSHIP BAROMETER

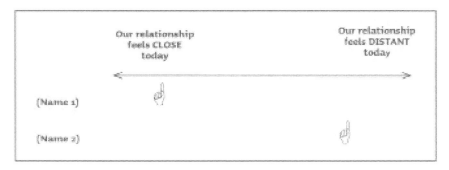

On a daily basis, or more often if you wish, move the arrow to indicate the level of closeness or distance you experience with your partner. Use this as an opportunity to talk openly about the closeness/distance you feel in your relationship.

TOOL #4: HOW HAVE I CREATED THIS EXPERIENCE?

Another tool for creating change in your relationship is to *take responsibility for whatever shows up in your life.* In effect, you become the Chief Executive Officer of your life. As the CEO you take responsibility, no matter what occurs.

One way to do this is by asking yourself the question, *"How have I created this experience in my life now?"*, and *"Now that this experience is happening in my life, what will I do about it?"*

By fully owning and taking responsibility for having created

<u>all</u> of the experiences in your life, you make yourself very powerful. Rather than acting as if you are a *victim* of your life, you assume the role of *creator* for your life.

In our experience, when a person accepts full responsibility for creating his/her life, they become very powerful and are able to effect amazing changes. They shift from a belief that life *happens to them*, to a belief that they *create all the experiences* in their lives. Imagine the shift that would occur if you asked yourself these two questions:

- How did I create this experience in my life?
- What do I intend to do about it?

Think of it this way: *<u>You</u> are the Knight in Shining Armor you've been waiting for!*

The implication of this expression is that there is no one but ourself to rescue us from life's events. Change is *up to us* to enact in our lives. By owning our lives and taking responsibility for whatever occurs, we move to a place of incredible power and influence in our own life story.

PAUSE AND PONDER

Think of an experience you previously assumed was outside of your control; something you assumed happened <u>to</u> you.

Now, for the sake of this exercise, consider this same

experience from the perspective of <u>you having created this experience</u> in your life. What might be the reason you created this? What might you do about it now?

   ⤜⤏ **The experience I wish to focus on is:**

   ⤜⤏ **How I created this experience is:**

   ⤜⤏ **The reason I created this experience is:**

✏ Now that I'm aware I created this experience, I intend to:

Here is an example to help demonstrate this concept. It is an actual event that occurred in Ted's life.

The experience I wish to focus on is:

Feeling hurt when my partner failed to organized a birthday party for me when I turned 40.

How I created this experience is:

I created this experience by not informing my partner of my desire to have a party to celebrate my 40th birthday. I also failed to inform my partner that I wanted her to organize the party for me as an expression of her love for me.

The reason I created this experience is:

To test my partner's love. To see if she really cared about me. To make my partner responsible for my happiness.

 318

Now that I'm aware I created this experience, I intend to:

Be clear with others about what I want in life. Address my desires and concerns directly. Take responsibility for creating my own happiness.

This way of engaging the world may seem odd to you at this time. Temporarily suspend your judgment about the 'rightness' or 'wrongness' of this idea and simply notice whether this way of engaging life works for you. Remember that the 'right answer' is the one that works *for you*. Does seeing yourself as the *creator* of your experiences help you to have a better relationship?

CREATION VS. REACTION

Do you know the difference between creation and reaction? Neil Donald Walsch, author of *Conversation With God: An Uncommon Dialogue*, offers the following perspective. He asks his readers to write the words *Creation* and *Reaction*, one word above the other, as follows:

Creation

Reaction

He then asks, "*What is the difference between these two words?*" His answer is that with creation, the C is first; whereas with reaction, the C comes later. He suggests that every act of creation requires that you 'C' first—that you see what you want to create, and then you take action. If you don't, you will end up simply reacting.

When you react in life, it's often because you don't see where you are going. As a result, you end up walking around in the dark, banging into things and reacting to the pain that results.

In order to experience life as a process of creation rather than reaction, stop and pause and see what you are doing, thinking, and feeling. *See what it is you want to create.*

TOOL #5: JOURNALING

To make changes to your relationship requires you take time regularly to notice what is working in your life and what isn't working. An effective tool for increasing your ability to notice is journaling. Journaling is the practice of pausing, noticing and recording your thoughts and feelings. The more often you journal, the more your skill of noticing will increase.

We encourage you to take time to stop and pause and journal about the life you are living. Julia Cameron, author of *The Artist's Way*, recommends the practice of writing what she calls 'morning pages'. (She also humorously calls them 'moaning' pages!)

Her advice is to write a minimum of three pages every morning. Then at the end of each week or each month, look back and take note of what you did and felt and thought.

This process may help to illuminate your way and make your life more an act of creation rather than reaction.

The unexamined life is not worth living.

Plato

TOOL #6: ASK FOR FEEDBACK

Another way to increase your ability to notice, is to invite your partner, family, and friends to share their observations about you, with you. Other people can be a valuable source of information. Sometimes others are better able to see who you are and what you are doing than you are.

An excellent method of exploring the different aspects of yourself in relationship is by using a model known as *Johari's Window.* It was created by Joseph Luft and Harrington Ingham in 1955 to help people better understand their relationship with self and others.

Think of our relationship with others as a house with four rooms. The first room is the part of ourselves that we see and others see. The second room shows the aspects that others see, but which we are not aware of.

The third room is the most mysterious room in that it contains the unconscious or subconscious part of us which is seen by neither ourselves nor others.

The final room is our private space, which we know but keep from others.

The benefit of Johari's Window is its ability to succinctly and visually depict the various aspects of self—the Open Self, Hidden Self, Blind Self, and Unknown Self. (See below)

JOHARI'S WINDOW

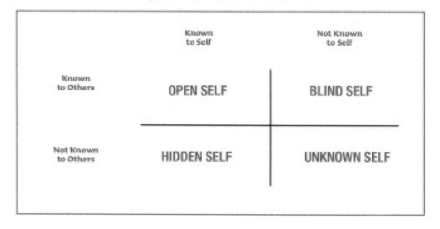

Open Self   =   Known to Self + Known to Others

        Hidden Self   =   Known to Self + Not Known to Others

        Blind Self   =   Not Known to Self + Known to Others

        Unknown Self   =   Not Known to Self + Not Known to Others

Significant to this discussion is the *Blind Self*. This is where information is known to others, but not to you. Others can often see aspects of ourselves that we are blind to. Only by relating with others and being open to the feedback of others, can our Blind Self become smaller, and our Open Self larger. Through feedback from others, you come to see and know your self more fully.

Others serve as a mirror for you. They have the ability to reflect back to you who you are and *how you are being* in life.

You can gather valuable information about yourself by considering the question, *"What is this person mirroring back to me about who I am?"*

CASE STUDY : JOHARI'S WINDOW

Ron and Teresa came for counseling to address Ron's anger. It seems Ron would have episodes of explosive anger two or three times per month, and the anger was causing damage to their relationship. Ironically, Ron was confused by his intense anger as he prided himself on normally being a fairly calm and logical person. Yet, each time the anger erupted, both Ron and Teresa would suffer the damage that resulted from the intensity and harshness of the anger.

"How much notice do you have that you will have explosive anger?" Ted asked Ron. Ron replied, *"About thirty seconds."*

Ted then turned to Teresa. *"And how much notice do you have that Ron will have one of his angry outbursts?"*

"About three days." Teresa responded.

Teresa could read the cues in Ron's tone of voice, the

stiffness in his body, and the increasing rigidity with which he engaged daily tasks. She could predict that an outburst was imminent, not unlike being able to predict that a tea-kettle will start whistling by noticing the increasing steam escaping from the spout.

Ron was surprised at Teresa's answer. "*Really?*" he asked. The thought that Teresa could predict a coming explosion was confusing to Ron. For him, the anger emerged suddenly and without notice.

It truly shocked him each and every time the anger erupted.

The challenge for Ron is he was almost completely unaware of his emotional body. Ron had never learned to acknowledge his emotions and notice where they sat in his body. Ron learned to manage life by relying on his intellect. His emotions and body sensations were a mystery to him.

Teresa, on the other hand, had become an expert in reading her emotions and that of others. She learned to read body cues—the color in one's cheeks, the tone of voice, and the ease or stiffness of the walk—as easily as one reads a newspaper.

Teresa needed to learn these skills as a way of keeping herself safe as a child.

Ted asked Ron if he would be willing to ask Teresa to be a resource in his life.

"*Would you be willing to utilize the expertise Teresa has acquired in being able to read emotions and body movements?*" Ted inquired.

"*What do you mean?*" asked Ron.

"Well," said Ted, "*it seems that Teresa is like an early warning detection system. She can read when your emotions are building and bring this to your awareness.*"

"*If you invite her to share her observations with you, she might be able to help you avoid the explosions of anger that are causing so much damage in your relationship.*"

Ted explained that it's easier to unravel emotions when they are still small. Ted likened this to the difference between climbing out of a hole that is six inches deep compared to one that is six feet deep.

"*The challenge,*" Ted said, "*is whether you are willing to invite Teresa to be a resource in managing this aspect of your life.*"

Ted went on to explain: "*Teresa isn't responsible for managing your emotions, however, she might be a valuable resource in helping you to manage your emotions by bringing information to your awareness that you aren't able to access at this time.*"

"*The key is that you need to ask for assistance.*"

In this example, Teresa was able to see aspects of Ron that he couldn't see himself. Ron's emotions and body sensations were contained in the 'Blind Self' quadrant.

With Teresa's assistance, Ron might be able to shrink his 'Blind Self' and increase the size of his 'Known Self'.

It all depends on whether he is willing to admit there is something he can't see, and invite the assistance of someone who can see.

TOOL #7: GET BACK TO YOUR SENSES

Change is often thwarted by fear. Fear is one of the largest obstacles to making changes in a relationship. Fear paralyzes. It causes you to freeze. Fear can prevent you from moving forward.

One way to overcome fear is to confront whatever it is you fear. In the light of day, fear often dissolves. Remember, *fear is always about the future* and using your imagination to imagine a negative outcome.

When you notice you are afraid, recognize you have moved into your future and are telling yourself a story with a negative outcome.

There are two ways to change your feelings of fear. One is to bring yourself into the present moment; to *live in the now*. An effective way to become fully present is to get back to your senses. You do this by intentionally activating your five senses.

When you consciously and intentionally activate either your sense of smell, touch, hearing, sight, or taste you move into the present because you must be in the present to intentionally receive the stimuli.

Smell a flower, touch some tree bark, hear the sounds of the birds, look intentionally at someone, put a piece of fruit in your mouth and consciously taste it.

Each of these behaviors will bring you back into the present moment. When you are in the present moment your fear will dissipate.

TOOL #8: TELL A NEW STORY

A second strategy to address fear is to tell yourself a new story, a story that has a positive outcome. Simply change the outcome of the story you are telling yourself. When a story has a positive outcome, we feel better. We move to a place of excitement, anticipation and hopefulness.

Given that it's the future we are dealing with, anything is possible. We can create whatever outcome we want. So why not tell yourself a nice story?

All of our emotional experiences are determined by the stories we tell ourselves. Learn to tell yourself nice stories—stories of success, growth, positive outcomes, intimacy, and love.

The importance of telling yourself good stories is wonderfully expressed in this First Nations story—the Story of Two Wolves.

THE STORY OF TWO WOLVES

When confronting your fears you might consider following the advice of a wise Native elder. His advice is contained in a story about a young man who was performing a rite of passage ritual.

The ritual required this young warrior to go on a journey into the wilderness where he was to care for himself for many days without assistance from anyone.

On the evening prior to embarking on his journey, the young man had a dream. In the dream he saw two wolves. One wolf spoke to him and said, "You won't make it. You will die on your journey."

The second wolf also spoke to him. This wolf said, "You are a strong and loving man and will become a great leader."

When the young man awoke the next morning he told his dream to an elder. He asked the elder, "Which wolf is telling me the truth?"

The elder replied, "The wolf that said you are strong and will become a great leader."

"How do you know?" asked the young man.

"Because", said the elder, "you will feed only one wolf. You will only feed the wolf that is positive."

Which 'wolf' do you feed? Do you feed the wolf that is positive and encouraging, or do you feed the wolf that is negative and discouraging?

Get good at telling yourself stories that motivate and encourage you in creating a better relationship. Be an inspiration to yourself.

TOOL #9: I AM LOVABLE

In our experience many people have a fear of intimacy. They are afraid that if their partner should get too close, he or she might be able to see their flaws and imperfections. At the root of this fear are the beliefs:

"I am unlovable as I am."

"I am not good enough the way I am."

"I am not worthy of your love and affection the way I am."

"There are things about me that make me unlovable."

A belief of being unlovable will undermine your efforts to create a more intimate relationship. That is why *worthiness* is one of the essential ingredients of an intimate relationship—as we discussed in Week **1**.

We have met many couples who were committed to improving their relationship, yet once they began to experience greater closeness, one or both would behave in ways that would push the other away.

From the outside, their behavior appears irrational. The behavior begins to make sense when we recognize the belief of being unlovable is undermining the desire for more intimacy.

Because people sometimes believe they are unlovable, they push away their partner before their partner notices their unlovable qualities and rejects them.

Take a moment to consider if this belief is present with you.

PAUSE AND PONDER

☞ **Do you fear intimacy at times? When?**

☞ **Do you sometimes think you are unlovable? When?**

✒ **What aspect of yourself do you think your partner hasn't yet seen which would cause them to reject you if they saw it?**

This fear of being unlovable is irrational. We are all lovable *just as we are*. Do you think every infant is worthy of love? Of course. So, at what point do you think an infant becomes unworthy of love?

No matter what your imperfections may be, you are still worthy of love. Tell yourself regularly, "*I am lovable just as I am.*" Nourish the belief of your lovability.

How could anyone ever tell you,
You were anything less than beautiful?
How could anyone ever tell you,
You were less than whole?
How could anyone fail to notice
That your loving is a miracle?
How deeply you're connected to my soul.

Lyrics from a spiritual song

TOOL #10: FORGIVENESS

One of the most important tools we can use to create a better relationship is *forgiveness*.

The ability to forgive others—and especially yourself—for any disappointments, is crucial to allowing you to move on in your life and not get stuck in old experiences.

Many people struggle with forgiveness. They assume forgiveness is something one does to 'aid' another, usually the person who has done them some perceived wrong. We believe forgiveness is actually *a gift to yourself.*

When you forgive, you release anger, resentment and other emotions that weigh heavily upon you. Forgiveness allows you to walk easier and lighter on your path in life.

When you learn that forgiveness is a gift to yourself, it becomes something you'll want to do easily and often.

Forgiveness has nothing to do with absolving
a criminal of his crime. It has everything to do
with relieving oneself of the burden of being a victim;
letting go of the pain and transforming oneself
from a victim to a survivor.

C.R. Strahan

TOOL #11: BREATHING

Most people don't give the act of breathing a second thought. They simply take it for granted. The reality is that most people breathe very poorly and inefficiently, using only the top of their lungs; and fail to exhale fully. They almost never engage the full capacity of their lungs. This is because most people don't breathe using their diaphragm.

When you breathe using your diaphragm, your belly (below your belt) will rise and fall. Notice how a baby breathes; watch its belly. And yet at some stage, usually as young children, we begin to breathe without the full use of our diaphragm. This is because we hold our bellies in. We think it is more attractive this way, and it is also due to our muscles tensing out of fear.

When you breathe using your diaphragm you will notice that you are calmer, more grounded, and more stable—physically, emotionally, and psychologically. Those who have been trained in traditional forms of martial arts or healing arts know the importance of breathing from your diaphragm.

It is also a wonderful way to calm yourself anytime you are feeling anxious. Simply close your eyes for a few moments and take several deep, complete breaths—that is, expel all the air in your lungs, forcing out every last drop.

Then breathe in very slowly through your nose to the count of ten, until your lungs are almost bursting. Force more air in. Then hold it for a slow count of ten.

Finally, breathe out slowly through your mouth for a count of ten.

Take a few normal breaths, and repeat several times. You will be amazed at how much calmer you feel.

It is said that, *"the way you breathe is the way you live your life"*. What this means is that if you breathe from the top of your lungs, you will be reactive and easily knocked over by the challenges of life. If you breathe from your diaphragm, you will be more grounded and able to live comfortably in your whole body rather than only in your intellect. Try it and see if you are able to notice the difference your breathing makes.

In addition to reducing your anxiety levels and helping bring you more fully into the present, remember that a peaceful, focused mind is one of the most precious gifts you can bring your beloved so you are fully present to the divine giftedness he/she offers you.

TOOL #12: WHAT WOULD LOVE DO NOW?

It is said there are only two emotions—love and fear. The most basic question of life is: Do you choose love or fear to flourish in your life?

If love is to flourish, you must make a commitment to love. Just like the story of the two wolves, you need to feed love and starve fear. You need to feed yourself with positive and loving thoughts. You need to take loving actions.

If you are wondering how to do this, the answer is simple: whenever you are required to make any decision or to take an action, ask yourself the question, *"What would love do now?"*

This question will always lead you in the direction of love. Focusing on love (remember the story of the race car driver) enhances your experience of love and of being loved in return. When you think and act in ways that are lovable, you experience yourself as lovable. You feel lovable.

If you want to feel love, give love to others. If you want to feel love, be vigilant with your fear.

Do not feed your fear. Do not allow it to flourish.

Refocus yourself onto the path of love.

The following poem expresses it well:

I Choose

To live by choice, not by chance.
To make changes, not excuses.
To be motivated, not manipulated.
To be useful, not used.
To excel, not compete.
I choose self-esteem, not self-pity.
I choose to listen to my inner voice
Not the random opinions of others.

TOOLS FOR CHANGE

We encourage you to review the following list of tools and make a commitment to use three of them over the next week to improve your relationship:

    ☞ **Tool #1:**   **Tell Your Truth**

    ☞ **Tool #2:**   **High-Low**

    ☞ **Tool #3:**   **Relationship Barometer**

    ☞ **Tool #4:**   **How Did I Create This Experience?**

    ☞ **Tool #5:**   **Journaling**

    ☞ **Tool #6:**   **Ask for Feedback**

    ☞ **Tool #7:**   **Get Back to Your Senses**

    ☞ **Tool #8:**   **Tell a New Story**

    ☞ **Tool #9:**   **I am Lovable**

    ☞ **Tool #10:**   **Forgiveness**

    ☞ **Tool #11:**   **Breathing**

    ☞ **Tool #12:**   **What would Love Do Now?**

WHICH TOOLS WILL YOU USE?

I am making a commitment to use at least the following 3 tools in the next week:

➵ Tool #_____: _____

➵ Tool #_____: _____

➵ Tool #_____: _____

THE END OF OUR 8-WEEK JOURNEY

And so, we have finally reached the conclusion of our 8-Week journey together. We hope you have learned some valuable lessons over this time, and trust that you have grown in many ways. We hope that you have many more tools in your personal toolbox to help you deal with the challenges of relationships, and it is our wish that you have experienced moments of greater intimacy, happiness and joy in your current relationship.

Alternatively, if this journey has led you to a realization that the most loving thing you can do for yourself and your partner is to move on to a better relationship with somebody else, we applaud you for your courage and sincerely hope your partner understands and appreciates the wisdom of your loving gesture.

EMBRACING A WIDER RELATIONSHIP

By joining us on this 8-Week journey, you have not only moved closer to a better relationship with your significant other, but have also learned valuable lessons that will benefit all of us on this planet.

As you learn and practice the skills of intimacy, truth telling, respecting differences, creating win-win solutions, and walking the path of love instead of fear, you become a valuable resource in making the whole world a better place.

When Gandhi was asked, *"How do you change the world?"* he replied, *"Become the change you want the world to be"*. As we change ourselves into more peaceful, loving and joyful beings, we spread this experience into the world.

We are like a pebble dropped into a pond. The pebble sends ripples throughout the pond. When we are pebbles of love and respect and peace, we send waves of love and respect and peace out into the pond that is our universe.

Go with love, fellow traveller.

 # THE END
(which is also the Beginning)

ABOUT THE AUTHORS, & THEIR PERSONAL 10 TIPS

There are a few people who truly, truly walk the talk.

Olympia Dukakis

A NEVER-ENDING JOURNEY

Building and maintaining a better relationship is a never-ending, moment-by-moment process... not just for you, but for us as well. As authors, we truly strive to walk our talk.

And so, we thought, what better way to end this book, than to share with you something about each of us, as well as our own individual top ten suggestions; the things we try to do each day with our own partners to build and maintain our relationships.

TED KUNTZ

Ted is a gifted psychotherapist and author of the best-selling book *Peace Begins With Me*. Ted has a Master's Degree in Counseling Psychology and more than 25 years' experience as a marriage and family therapist and a consultant. He is an avid writer and has contributed to both local and national media, and is also a contributing author to *The Thought That Changed My Life Forever*. His monthly blog is entitled *Peace Begins With Me – Ideas and Inspiration*. Ted has been recognized internationally for his work in assisting individuals, families, organizations, and corporations manage the challenges, opportunities, and stresses of life more effectively and joyfully. Ted lives with his wife in Vancouver. To access Ted's website and blog visit: www.peacebeginswithme.ca

TED'S LISTS

What I do that Makes a Difference:

- Share a coffee in the morning and discuss our day.
- Spend time together at night and review our day.
- Disconnect the TV.

- Go for walks and bicycle rides.

- Have a couple only date night every two weeks.

- Laugh. Tease. Play.

- Not take anything personally.

- Take 100% responsibility for my thoughts, feelings and behaviors.

- Buy flowers.

- Vacuum our home.

What My Wife does that Makes a Difference:

- Makes a lovely meal with what I like in mind.

- Cuddles with me on the couch.

- Laughs at my jokes.

- Is happy to see me when I come home from work.

- Puts toothpaste on my toothbrush.

- Holds my hand when we walk.

- Sends me cute emails when she is away.

- Pours my coffee and brings it to me.

- Goes for walks with me.

- Takes 100% responsibility for her thoughts, feelings and behaviors.

ROWAN JOHNSON

Rowan Johnson has degrees in Psychology, an MA in Applied Linguistics and English Language Teaching from the University of Nottingham, England, and is currently teaching writing and completing his doctorate at the University of Chattanooga, Tennessee. He has published various forms of writing, including novels, essays, poetry and flash fiction. Some of his work has been published in Wordriver Literary Review and the 2012 Writers Abroad Foreign Encounters Anthology. He has also written numerous travel articles for publications such as The Complete Woman and SEOUL Magazine in South Korea where he lived for several years. Born in South Africa, Rowan has traveled the world extensively and lived and

worked in Canada and South Korea, and currently resides with his wife Sybil in the United States.

ROWAN'S LIST

What we Both do that Makes a Difference:

- Read each others' writing and make lots of comments and suggestions.
- Constantly discuss how things are going in our relationship.
- Make firm plans for future activities that increase our daily happiness.
- Maintain strong family relationships with both sets of relatives.
- Ask each other before accepting or declining invitations to events.
- Keep our house neat and tidy.
- Avoid badmouthing each other in front of anybody else.
- Take care to maintain our physical health and appearance.
- Have fun! Often go to restaurants, festivals, bars and concerts together.
- Travel the world graciously and fully accept each others' habits and lifestyles.

LEE JOHNSON

Lee is a writer and ghostwriter with degrees in English and Psychology, and author of several books including the Penguin Books #1 bestseller *How To Escape Your Comfort Zones* which topped the best-seller lists for 8 consecutive weeks. His diverse career includes teacher, therapist, professional rock musician, and heading up the creative departments for some of the world's leading advertising agencies, winning many awards including 8 international Clios. He also wrote two stage musicals including *The Ancient Mariner* starring Oliver Reed and Michael York, an animated children's TV series *Balltown* that teaches universal values and life skills to young children, and over a hundred recorded songs. Born in South Africa, Lee currently lives in Vancouver, Canada. Visit his website at www.leejohnsonwriter.com.

LEE'S LIST

What we Strive to do Individually and Together that Makes a Difference:

- Getting up early in the morning (easy for me!) to make coffee, then sharing a cup together and discussing whatever is important to each of us and both of us.

- Building and maintaining trust through complete transparency and honesty: sharing our dreams as well as our nightmares; our hopes as well as our fears; our successes as well as our failures

- Giving time and doing supportive things to make each other's lives easier, and appreciating that these things are much more important than giving 'stuff'.

- Surprising each other periodically with unusual dates: fried chicken picnic in the park, a glass of wine on the beach watching the sunset, music in a Chinese garden.

- Supporting each other in going to the gym, watching what we eat, helping each other through tough times but resisting the urge to rescue, knowing that embracing the experience is usually Life's best teacher.

- Doing lots of fun things together: strolling along the seawall, taking the dog for a walk in the forest, a night at the theatre for ballet or a play, escaping for a romantic weekend, just being with each other enjoying Nature or watching TV without feeling the need to talk.

- Listening with all our senses and resisting the urge to interject or comment or pass judgment.

- Nurturing family ties and mutual friendships by consciously spending quality time with each of them.

- Accepting that neither of us can ever be perfect and being truly grateful for all our wonderful and unique gifts.

- Constantly striving individually and helping each other to become better people, knowing that who we truly are is more important than what others may think of us.

NOW WRITE YOUR OWN LIST:

This can be a list acknowledging what your partner does, or listing what you do, or both. It may also be a 'wish list' of things you would like to do, or have done. Have fun!

BIBLIOGRAPHY:

*If it seems we have vision,
it is only because we sit
on the shoulders of giants.*

Isaac Newton

Branden, N. (1985): *The Psychology of Romantic Love.*
Bantam Books.

Cameron, J. (2002): *The Artist's Way: A Spiritual Path to Higher Creativity.*
Putnam.

Chapman, G. (1992): *The Five Love Languages: How to Express Heartfelt Commitment to Your Mate.*
Northfield Publishing.

Covey, S. R. (1989). *The Seven Habits of Highly Effective People.*
Free Press.

Donald Walsch, N. (1996): *Conversations With God: An Uncommon Dialogue.*
G. P. Putnam's Sons.

Dyer, W. (2004): *The Power of Intention.*
Hay House Inc.

Frankl, V. E. (1959): *Man's Search for Meaning.*
Beacon Press.

Gayle West, M. (2000): *Exploring the Labyrinth: A Guide for Healing and Spiritual Growth.*
Three Rivers Press.

Gray, J. (1992): *Men Are from Mars, Women Are from Venus.*
Harper Collins.

Hendrix, H (1988): *Getting the Love You Want.*
Harper-Perennial.

Hillman, J. (2010): *A Blue Fire - Selected Writings* By James Hillman.
Harper-Perennial.

Johnson, L. and Koopman, A. (1995): *How to Escape your Comfort Zones.*
Penguin Books.

Kuntz, T. (2005): *Peace Begins With Me*.
Friesens Press.

Miguel Ruiz, D. (1997): *The Four Agreements: A Practical Guide to Personal Freedom*.
Amber-Allen Publishing.

Rose Kingma, D. (1999): *The Future of Love*.
Main Street Books.

Tolle, E. (2004): *The Power of Now: A Guide to Spiritual Enlightenment*.
New World Library.

Vanzant, I. (1998): *One Day My Soul Just Opened Up: 40 Days and 40 Nights Toward Spiritual Strength and Personal Growth*.
Touchstone.

Guinette, C. and Roberts, G. (2012): *The Thought That Changed My Life Forever*.
The Thought Publications/Morgan James.

Woollam, R. H. (1985): *On Choosing with a Quiet Mind*.
Unica Publishing.

Woollam, R. H. (1989): *Have a Plain Day*.
Unica Publishing.

Zukav, G. (1990): *The Seat of the Soul*.
Free Press.

NOTES: